Britain on the Brink

Britain on the Brink

Edited by Martyn Eden

Crossway Books
Nottingham

ISBN 1 85684 048 4

Unless otherwise stated, Scripture quotations in this publication are from
the Holy Bible, New International Version. Copyright © 1973, 1978,
1984 International Bible Society. Published in Great Britain by Hodder
& Stoughton Ltd.

Typeset by Avocet Typesetters, Bicester, Oxon
Printed in Great Britain for Crossway Books, Norton Street, Nottingham
NG7 3HR

Contents

Introduction

A newspaper article in September 1991 declared that 'the traditional family (two parents plus their children) is a thing of the past'. The writer drew this conclusion from a Gallup poll which revealed the following analysis of British households:

traditional family household	25%
single person household	26%
single parent household	9%
married or cohabiting/no children	36%
other households	4%

Another report also published in 1991, showed that Britain has the highest percentage of one-parent families in Europe. One in seven (14%) of all British families with children are one-parent families. The percentage of British children born out of wedlock also continues to rise. In 1989, 42% of all conceptions and 29.2% of all births were to unmarried women. Only one in ten of the single women who become pregnant now marry before giving birth.

50% of all British couples who marry in their twenties have lived together beforehand, compared with 5% in the 1960s. However, cohabitation does not appear to be leading to more stable marriages, for divorce continues to increase. More than one in three marriages now end in divorce, with more than half of these having a child under 16.

These statistics give us a partial impression of how the British family is changing. For a complete picture, a lot more information, both qualitative and quantitative, would be needed. But even on the basis of what is here, most Christian readers will be drawing pessimistic conclusions. The Church has traditionally followed the Bible in placing a high value on monogamous, lifelong marriages; the containment of sex within marriage; and children being born into and brought up within a stable family. So, is the impression these statistics give us one that sees Britain on the brink of a social and moral catastrophe?

Not everyone would think so. Opinion polls reveal that 62% of the general public see nothing wrong with cohabitation before marriage. 57% do not think that couples should stay together if their marriage has broken down. There is also evidence that 22.8% of the single mothers have actively chosen that state. Evidently, many of those who stay away from the churches every Sunday have also rejected Christian ethical traditions. How should Christians respond to this? Should we concern ourselves only with those who share our faith or should we be seeking to influence the direction of social trends in order to restore the influence of Christian values in British society?

Such questions are the focus of this book. Where is Britain going at the end of the twentieth century? And what should be our responses? The contributors share a desire to help God's people to understand the signs of our times in order to make a positive impact on society so that it becomes more pleasing and acceptable to God. Too often in the recent past, we seem to have woken up to social trends when they were already upon us. We may proclaim an almighty God but we often give the impression of being powerless before the apparently relentless advance of secularisation. Yet, as we examine the consequences, such as those reported above, it is difficult to believe that they mean fulfilment and wholeness for those who have embraced secular values. Do not those who by God's grace recognise this, have a duty to persuade society to change direction? But before we can do that we have first to understand the current trends in British society or we shall merely continue the dialogue of the deaf that has characterised much evangelistic and social endeavour in recent years.

There are those who say that, such is the state of our nation, the only thing British Christians can and should do now is to engage in evangelism. It is certainly true that unbelievers need to hear the Gospel and receive God's gift of salvation through faith in Christ but this is easier said than achieved. Tragically, despite numerous national and local missions in recent years, 90% of the adult British population have not accepted the gift. Is this because they have consciously rejected Christ? Or is it because they were being offered something they did not realise they needed, in a vocabulary they did not comprehend, by evangelists who seemed indifferent to needs the unbelievers knew they had? If this book helps to equip Christians to bridge these barriers by increasing understanding of contemporary social trends, one of our purposes will have been fulfilled.

It also has to be said that the view that personal evangelism should be our exclusive concern falls short of being the full message of the Bible. That message includes a strong theme, which runs right through Scripture, that God's people have responsibilities in the world as well as in His Kingdom. Put another way, we have a mission to our culture and society as well as to individuals. This can be seen as early as Genesis 1:28, where God mandates His human creatures to subdue the earth and to rule. The subsequent Fall diminished our capacity for carrying out this responsibility but it has never been withdrawn. Christians who deny social responsibilities and leave them to others are implying that they are unwilling to serve in the world as God's stewards. When God called out Israel to be a holy people, set apart for Him, He did not relieve them of responsibilities in the world. On the contrary, they were to be 'a light to lighten the Gentiles'. Israel was not to be concerned only with its own. The Mosaic Law required them to care for the stranger and when they failed to do this they were roundly denounced by God's prophets.

The same theme, of God's people having responsibilities in the world, is also found in the New Testament. Jesus' disciples were to be salt and light; consistently different from the world but thoroughly mixed up in it to deter rottenness and to dispel darkness. The Good Samaritan similarly models responsibility for needy neighbours, even if they do come from a different culture or religion. The injunction to 'render to Caesar' and the picture of judgement in Matthew 25:31–46, both point in the same direction. Christians are not to hide in a pietistic ghetto but to be out in the world, living the values of the Kingdom and reflecting the character of our God. This will make us very different from the world but nonetheless very much belonging in it. And if Britain is on the brink of moral decay, the need for Christian salt and light is very great.

However, good intentions are not enough. It is important that we are not only well informed about what is happening in our society but that we also understand this from a Biblical perspective. For example, it would be very easy to be led by an examination of social trends into despair. The evidence cited above concerning the breakdown of the traditional family is deeply distressing to those who see the family as part of God's plan for maintaining stable societies. But the social changes that underlie this evidence are neither random nor inevitable. The Bible teaches with great force that God is sovereign. He allows people and nations to choose their direction and to live with the consequences but there is always the possibility of repentance and a turning back. He always has the last word. No social trend is irreversible. So, if God's people prayerfully determine to be effective salt and light, there are solid Biblical grounds for confidence that we can make a difference.

The way we understand history also influences how we respond to social change. Secular humanists·are prone to see history as a continuing movement towards progress. Thus recent developments and new institutions must be superior to those of the 'bad old days'. This is a very optimistic view of social change: some would say naive. A more pessimistic view is the cynical view which sees history as repeating itself. We are on a treadmill and there is no genuine basis for hope. We are bound to repeat the same old mistakes. As the poet, Steve Turner, has put it humorously,

> History repeats itself.
> Has to.
> No one listens.

Christian thinkers have for the most part rejected both these views and adopted a linear view of history which offers grounds for hope without being blind to the influence of sin and evil. In the language of Scripture this linear process begins with creation, incorporates the fall and the redemptive work of Jesus, and will end with the second coming and judgement. Within this perspective, social trends can be appraised in relation to God's purposes, revealed in creation and the redemptive dynamic of His Kingdom, which Jesus inaugurated. In very crude terms, we ask how a particular change fits with 'the maker's plans'.

But we need to be careful not to confuse the prejudices derived from a particular cultural experience with God's intentions. Thus, before British Christians identify the nuclear family as the creation model we need to ask how Christians in other ages and cultures have understood and applied Biblical teaching on the family.

The ultimate source of hope in the Biblical view of history lies in the recognition that God will have the last word. However depressing we may find particular social trends, if the Bible is truly God's revelation, then we know how all things will end. Moreover, when we see developments that seem to reflect human sinfulness, we understand what is happening and we do not panic. But this understanding gives us a responsibility. It is to be God's called-out people in this time, place and situation, reading the signs of the times and responding to them in a way that honours Him.

That is the common aim which has brought together the very diverse group of contributors to this volume. We come from a variety of backgrounds and we feel strongly about quite different issues. Nevertheless, between us we hope to increase understanding of current trends in British society and motivate our fellow evangelicals to respond Biblically to them. Nowhere is this more necessary than in relation to Britain's membership of the European Community.

There are some very odd attitudes towards Europe nurtured amongst British Evangelicals. As the Iron Curtain came down, there was a headlong rush to carry the Gospel into the East but a puzzling indifference to the spiritual condition of Western Europe, where secularisation has bitten deeply into so many of the national cultures. Even more distressing is the insensitive, some would say arrogant, way in which outreach has sometimes been conducted. Too often, the emphasis has been on what we can do for them without any apparent awareness of what we can learn from Churches who have endured 70 years of oppression.

Equally perplexing are those who remain obdurately opposed to British involvement in the Community on allegedly Biblical grounds. Whilst it is perfectly reasonable to be critical of the Community's performance in specific areas, such as the common agricultural policy or the Community's effects on the two-thirds world, it is neither reasonable nor honouring to God to interpret verses in the book of Revelation in a narrowly Eurocentric way, to claim that the EC is a creature of the Anti-Christ. Disinformation about the European Community does not come only from fundamentalist sources, of course. Secular opponents of our EC membership have also contributed their share. Sir Fred Catherwood is highly qualified to deal with these inaccuracies. As a senior MEP and a former Vice President of the European Parliament, he is able to write from firsthand experience of trends and events. He demolishes current myths about the EC and confronts the reader with some numbing questions. What happens if democracy does not work in Eastern Europe? What is there to prevent a recurrence of militant nationalism if we fail to make the European Community work?

One consequence of such failures would almost certainly be additional threats to religious liberties, which cannot be taken for granted even today, as Mike Morris makes clear in his chapter. He reports the alarming statistics of martyrdom every month and explains the causes of religious intolerance. The picture looks bleak but there are things we can do to make a difference. Martyn Eden reaches a similar conclusion in chapter 3 on domestic political trends. He examines where the present government is trying to lead us, against the background of underlying social currents. He is unhappy with what this reveals but says we have only ourselves to blame. Salt that remains in the salt cellar flavours nothing: Christians who hide in a religious ghetto cannot complain when secular politics leaves an unpalatable taste. To make a difference we have to root our politics in Biblical principles as thoroughly and as consistently as secularists act on theirs.

The family is a case in point, as the evidence marshalled earlier demonstrates. Yet, our experience of family is so much a part of who we are that it is not easy to reflect objectively on current trends. Joan King helps us to overcome this by eavesdropping on the family life of Jenny and Graham. They are celebrating their golden wedding anniversary and as they prepare for a big family party they ponder the changes over four generations. On Sunday they will thank God for their fifty years together and as their minister prepares his address, he reflects theologically on contemporary changes to family life. The difficult questions which confront him challenge us too.

From family we turn to youth. Is there such a thing as youth culture and what can we learn about it that would enable us to better understand young people? Arkle Bell has recently complemented his extensive youth work experience with academic research and he draws on both in this chapter. His conclusions will surprise and disturb many but given the rate at which young adults are abandoning the Church they deserve our close and prayerful attention.

One of the strongest influences on young people is their eleven or more years of compulsory education. George Oliver expertly guides us through current educational trends. He examines the central features of the education process and exposes a secular drift within them. How do we respond to this as parents, as Christian teachers and school governors and as churches? The reader is offered some thoughtful suggestions, reinforced by resources for follow-up action.

When the issues to be addressed in this book were first considered, it seemed important to include what is happening amongst our brothers and sisters in the Black-led and Asian churches. Joel Edwards outlines the history of the Afro Caribbean community in Britain and opens some windows into the current state of and trends in the Black Church community. Pradip Sudra does the same with regard to the British Asian scene. There are some hard lessons to be learnt from the past but there are also grounds for encouragement and a vision of one people united in worship of the Lamb.

The growing popularity of alternatives to the Gospel, about which Ernest Lucas writes, points to one area in which we have much to learn from our Asian brothers and sisters. Eastern religions have been a powerful influence on many of these alternatives and nobody knows better than Asian Evangelicals how to handle them and reach their followers with the Gospel. Dr Lucas begins with plain, old-fashioned hedonism and traces the connecting threads through materialism to humanism and 'man'-centred religions. Predictably, these have failed to deliver what they promised and the disenchanted have turned eastward and come upon the New Age Movement. This will prove to be just as hollow but Dr Lucas calls the Church to ask itself why so many are turning to such a spurious counterfeit rather than to Christ.

Since these chapters are addressed primarily to the Evangelical constituency, it seemed appropriate to ask Clive Calver, the General Director of the Evangelical Alliance, to write the final chapter on 'The Evangelicals'. He writes of a 'peculiar people', frequently misunderstood by the rest of society. He looks back to the roots of evangelicalism to identify the core distinctives and demonstrates where these are at odds with contemporary trends. He examines how these key components of belief are to affect how we live in the future and challenges evangelicals to adapt without compromising our distinctives, in order to reach a culture which is moving further and further away from Christ.

Readers may question this selection of topics and regret some omissions. There is obviously a limit to what can be included in one book and sadly contributions on demographic and economic trends did not reach the finishing tape in time. In any case, there is no shortage of books on most of the topics which have not been covered.

The aim of this collection of short essays is to stimulate thought, prayer, discussion and, sooner or later, appropriate action. Though each of the contributors has expertise in their field, none would pretend that everything that could be said has been said in such short pieces. Nor is it expected that every reader will agree with all that has been written. But it is our hope that evangelicals, when they have read and pondered what is said about where Britain is heading, will be motivated by the Holy Spirit to get together with others to try to change these trends and reclaim Britain for Christ.

1

Britain and Europe

Sir Fred Catherwood

The last few years have not been kind to those in the business of forecasting trends in Europe. No one foresaw the collapse of Communism, the rise of democracy in Central and Eastern Europe, or the weakening of the other super power as America turned, inside a decade, from the world's greatest creditor nation to its greatest debtor. Nor did anyone foresee that to fill this vacuum the twelve Member States of the European Community would move so quickly towards a common Foreign and Security Policy and a common currency or that they would give such additional powers to their one common democratic institution, the European Parliament.

So those of us asked to write on trends in Europe must not be too dogmatic and must look first at what has happened.

Few Christians could have foreseen that our prayers for the persecuted churches of Central and Eastern Europe would have been so dramatically answered or foreseen the freedom of religion right across Europe from Cape Trafalgar to the Urals – and, beyond that, to Vladivostock and the Sea of Japan.

The world of the superpowers has now collapsed. The Soviet

Union has gone and the Americans, desperately short of cash, are taking their armies home. Europe is finding its feet again and its only organised political expression, the European Community, is expected to step into the breach.

Nearest home, the members of the European Free Trade Association are queuing up to join the Community. Austria, Sweden and Finland have applied, the Norwegian Prime Minister has said that Norway should follow and the Conservative opposition support her. Even the Swiss leaders are considering how they can get a referendum majority for Swiss membership. For the rest of Europe, the Community is the only show in town.

On the Community's eastern borders, Hungary, the Czech Republic and Poland want to join as soon as they are strong enough and an Association Agreement with each of them has already been signed as a half-way house.

The addition of the five rich countries of the European Free Trade Association, followed in a few years by the three much poorer Central European countries, would bring the Community to about 340 million, and that would, I think, be its practicable limit. If the Community is to keep the political cohesion needed to achieve its existing aims and especially if it is to give stability to the wider Europe and in the Mediterranean, it cannot grow any bigger. To achieve even that size it will have to improve its decision-making process, making it even more open and more democratic.

But, we may well ask, will it work? Can any superstate, in this fallible world, work for long?

There are already, of course, countries bigger than an enlarged Community. China has over a billion people, India 600 million, the United States 250 million, Brazil 150 million, Indonesia 180 million, Japan 125 million, and Pakistan, Bangladesh and Nigeria are all over 100 million.

It could fairly be argued that the United States is the only country approaching the Community's new size of anything like the same complexity. But I do not believe that a European Union will ever be a superstate. It is not its intention and, if it were, the existing states would frustrate it. They are far larger than the states of the USA and far older. They have effective and experienced national parliaments and national civil services and, above all, they have no common language. You cannot have a centralised democratic government if the voters cannot read each other's press or understand each other's radio and TV.

In any case, it is not the Community's intention to be a superstate. The Community's declared aim is to help its member states to act together for those individual and collective benefits which we would not be able to achieve if we acted separately. But for everything else the policy (called, in Eurospeak, 'subsidiarity') is to take decisions as near to the citizen as possible.

Perhaps the most important point for Christians to consider is whether we *want* it to work. Are its objectives our objectives?

Peace

The first objective of the Community is to create peace in place of Europe's terrible tribal wars, the last two of which cost 50 million dead.

For nearly half a century this objective has been achieved and we should not take it for granted. There has been genuine reconciliation, especially between Germany and France. But with the fighting and instability in Central and Eastern Europe, and the recent rise of right-wing nationalist parties in Western Europe, we cannot now take that peace for granted.

It is not enough for Christians to hope and pray for peace, we have to deal – as citizens – with the attitudes and conflicts of interest which lead to war.

We are told by Christ to be peacemakers and to love our neighbours as ourselves. Our Lord answered the question, Who is my neighbour? by the parable of the Good Samaritan, the neighbouring race which the Jews despised. If Christ were in England today he would preach the parable of The Good Frenchman.

So we, as Christians, should promote the institutions which promote peace between neighbours and settle conflicts by mutual agreement, the European Parliament, Council, Commission and Court.

Democracy

I believe that we should also, as Christians, support another aim of the Community, the development and extension of democracy. The Apostles lay down even fewer guidelines for civil government than they do for church government. But the Christian view of the dignity of men and women made in the image of God shines through everything. The Messiah was a carpenter, the Apostles were fishermen. Christ cares for the lowest in society. Everyone answers personally to him as Judge for all they have done and said.

Democracy makes the rulers take notice of everyone and that lends dignity to everyone. It also takes into account the corruption of power and makes it accountable to those who are ruled. Whatever its defects – for 'all men are sinners' – it reflects a Christian view of men and women, far better than the autocracies of the world.

So I see democracy as part of common grace, founded in the countries of the Reformation and developed slowly until, in the second half of this century, it has spread over Europe and is the aim of almost every people in this world. In the Community it is not only the aim, it is an absolute condition of membership. One of the greatest achievements of the Maastricht Treaty was the decisive (if not final) move towards democracy in the decision-making process of the Community itself, giving the elected Parliament, meeting and voting in public, more equal power with the diplomatic-dominated Council of Ministers, which meets behind closed doors, where the ministers who come on flying visits are told by their 'Sir Humphries' about the agreements reached with the eleven other Sir Humphries.

'Of course it's up to you minister, but if you follow this line I think you won't find any difficulty'.

Not much wonder when a junior minister follows the wise guidance of an experienced diplomat, he is a little shy when facing his national parliament and all is put through there late at night or on a Friday when no one much is around.

Now we hope, with equal powers in most legislation for the European Parliament, it will all be in the open where the public can hear and the press report the arguments so that the citizens can tell their elected members what they think.

We should not underestimate the Community's impact on the spread of democracy. Its insistence that only democracies can become members has undoubtedly influenced the change from autocracy to democracy in Greece, Spain and Portugal. The example of the Community, filtering across the Iron Curtain on TV and radio, ensured that Communism in Central and Eastern Europe was replaced by democracy and not by another dictatorship. And the Community has actively supported the spread of democracy in other parts of the world, especially in South America. The United States alone has not achieved what Europe and America have achieved together.

An honest currency

We may not think that monetary union is a moral issue or, if it is, that the moral centres on the defence of the British interest and the retention of the Queen's head on the coinage.

But there *is* a moral issue. It is inflation. Since the Queen's head first went on the currency it has lost nine-tenths of its value, a rate of inflation never before known in this country and totally without the excuse of the famine or war which have caused previous and lesser inflations.

Inflation is an arbitrary tax on rich and poor alike, but its effect has usually been to transfer wealth and income from the have-nots to the haves, from the weak to the strong, from those on the dole to those in work and, by putting a huge arbitrary spanner in the works of national economic management, it has put millions out of work.

During the Eighties, Britain's inflation and interest rates were double those of the Germans and Dutch and 50% more than the French, Danes, Irish, Belgians and Italians because in 1979 they had linked their currencies to the European Monetary System, the anchor of which was the German Mark, which was controlled, not by the German Government, but by their central bank, the Bundesbank.

Because the German Central Bank, the Bundesbank, is

controlled under the German Constitution by the central banks of Germany's regions, it is independent of the German Government. So when the German unions and employers negotiated pay deals they know – unlike *British* unions and management – that the central government cannot bail them out of the cost of excessive awards by printing money.

Since Britain linked the pound to the European Monetary System in October 1990, British inflation has already, at the time of writing, come down from 10% to 4% and interest rates from 15% to 10%.

But at Maastricht the twelve member governments decided that, with the inclusion in the system of Britain, Spain (and now Portugal) the system had to be strengthened and made less dependent on the Germans. And the wave of strikes in Germany five months later underlined that need.

So Monetary Union, they believed, should create a system similar to that of the Germans with an independent monetary authority to give us, once more, an honest currency which does not lose its value.

As for sovereignty over the pound, Britain has not had any since I went into public life in the early Sixties and, were I the Queen, I'd have long since removed my head in protest from the devalued coinage.

There are other objectives of the Community which we, as Christians, should support, the great efforts against pollution in the atmosphere, on our land, in lakes and rivers and on our beaches; the extensive and highly organised aid programme for developing countries, the sharp watch on human rights, the effort in the 1992 programme to promote trade between Member States and bring down unemployment, and the commitment by the richer states to help the poorer under the regional aid programme.

If there is one European issue which has long been nearest the heart of Christians, it was the oppression of the churches by the Communist regimes in Central and Eastern Europe.

Now the churches there are not only free, but there is a tremendous demand at all levels of society to know more of the faith which has been banned for generations. The pastors want books of theology, not least to counter the arguments of the flood of lavishly-funded sects. The academics want to understand the faith which has been central to European thought, law and social behaviour for nearly two thousand years. The governments say that the Communists have left them a people without any moral teaching – and the churches are full.

How long that state of affairs lasts depends on us.

Everyone who comes to see us in the European Parliament, Yeltsin from Russia, Walesa from Poland, Havel from Czechoslovakia, Antall from Hungary, emphasise that they are racing against time. If they cannot, within a few years, deliver economic stability, they cannot ensure political stability.

'Some messiah will come and tell the people that democracy does not work and they must follow him. So if you do not use your peace dividend to help us now, you will then have to put back on the frontier all the missiles, tanks, troops and aircraft you are now removing'.

In the late 1940s the United States gave Europe $70 billion over three years to recover from World War Two. Academic studies and a recent UN report show that far more is needed even than the generous Marshall Aid.

Marshall aid helped a Western Europe which had entrepreneurs who knew how to buy and sell in an open market, industrialists who knew how to make what people want to buy, banks who knew a good loan prospect from a bad one, Civil Servants who knew how to translate political decisions into laws and directives which were effective, and export managers who spoke their customers' languages. In Central and Eastern Europe all these people need to be trained from the beginning. And even if we cannot help them quite as intensively as the Germans are helping the East Germans, we still need to do far more in personal training and help on the spot – and all that costs money.

Their infrastructure, like their industry, is clapped out, idle for lack of spares and replacement. Russia, desperately in need of hard currency, cannot export oil because the pumps don't work and the pipes leak. The harvest in Ukraine cannot get to the northern cities because transport and storage is hopelessly inadequate and, even if they had, the Russians don't have the oil exports to trade for the grain.

There is continuing inflation because currency reserves are

exhausted and backing for the new currencies is inadequate.

And, in these conditions and without a commercial law on which they depend, investors from the west are reluctant to commit the capital and share the know-how, without which the eastern industries cannot begin to export.

There is no point in hoping that native capitalism will find a way through. It might, given a politically impossible ten or twenty years and tolerance of starvation meantime.

What is needed – and quickly – is a massive organised and heavily funded aid package with the best civil servants and industrialists on loan to run it. But that will not happen unless we, the citizens of Western Europe, insist that our governments act.

Materialism

But here we run head-on into one of the malign trends which could derail the whole European enterprise – materialism. A secular society believes that all we will ever have is the here and now and that there is no future life, and certainly no judgement. So, logically, it wants what it can get and wants to enjoy it as soon as it can in case it is too late. So it is very hard for governments to raise taxes to help the needy, even though the ultimate benefits are great and the risks of failure are horrendous.

It was materialism in the Eighties which wiped out America's surplus and landed that great country in chronic deficit. In Europe, it is the Germans alone who are giving anything like the levels of aid required. But though the East Germans are their people and Germany is in the front line, the Germans resent the higher taxes.

If we, as Christians, want to preserve the new-found freedom of the churches in those countries to the millions who now want to know all about our faith, the biggest open unevangelised field we are ever likely to find in our lifetime, then we should insist that the Community governments get moving.

Meantime we should give, while the opportunity is there. Four years ago money for Christians in Communist countries was easy to raise. Now, because everyone thinks the problem of religious freedom has been solved, it is much harder. Before it was difficult, under the Communist regime, to find causes on which churches would be allowed to spend the money. Now the need far outstrips the supply.

And we should pray for the higher level economic aid which is needed to undergird democracy and religious freedom. The Lord who answered our prayers for their freedom so dramatically can answer our prayers for the help their democratic governments need if they are to remain free.

Nationalism

The fighting in Sarajevo seemed to bring us, full circle, back to 1914 when the great powers of Europe quarrelled over the break-up of the Ottoman Empire and marched out, each under their national flag, to fight each other to the death. Four years later, 15 million had died. Twenty-five years later they quarrelled again over the break-up of the Austrian Empire, marched out again and, six years later, 35 million more had died. A Common Foreign and Security Policy is absolutely necessary to make sure that we do not fight each other over the break-up of the Russian Empire. The loose arrangements of the Maastricht Treaty are a step in the right direction, but not nearly enough.

Two generations on from the last war, nationalism is rising again. German, French and Belgian elections have increased the vote of nationalist parties, nationalism is tearing Yugoslavia apart and Yeltsin's proposals for a Commonwealth of Independent States look more and more difficult as Armenia fights Azerbaijan and Ukraine quarrels with Russia.

Europe's problem is that we have replaced the powerful populist nationalism with the secular humanism which is fast displacing the Christian faith in the intellectual leadership of European society. But it is an elitist creed. It has the power to weaken the pillars of society, especially the family, but it has no popular following.

So militant nationalism is not going to be put down by the wagging fingers of secular society. It can only be contained by a Christian faith and church which transcends race and nation and which sets its own imprint on culture and social behaviour.

The Christian faith teaches patriotism, the duty of every citizen to the government. But our teaching is against the nationalism which sets race against race and people against people. Christ was born into a strongly nationalist society; but he was explicitly found 'not guilty' of nationalism by its chief opponent, the Roman Governor. Pilate said, 'I find no fault in this man' and only when the Jews threatened to denounce him to Caesar as being soft on nationalism did he deliver Jesus to them for crucifixion.

The Apostle Paul laid it down that there was to be no barrier of race or class in the Christian Church, which should transcend all those barriers. We Christians should throw all our weight behind the effort to live peaceably with our neighbours; we should strengthen our links with churches in countries in which the Evangelical churches are weak, and we should take no part in the jingoism at home which sneers at all foreigners.

The nightmare scenario is a confrontation between the intellectual elite and the populist racialist mob.

This is not just a continental nightmare, though it might happen there first. It could happen in Britain too, especially with the break-up of the family and the arrival of an unloved and unloving generation with a grudge against the elite whose social experiments have so dismally failed.

The intellectuals preach tolerance, but only on the basis that we tolerate everything because nothing is true and all is relative. To preach that kind of tolerance to the nationalist is like spitting in the wind.

We preach a tolerance which comes from strength. We want freedom of speech for the Christian message because we believe – and have every reason to believe – that in a free exchange of views, it will prevail.

We believe in the power of the Holy Spirit to support our message, so we do not need the suppression of other faiths. The power which brought the Ethiopian eunuch to Jerusalem, Cornelius the Centurion to send for the Apostle Peter, Lydia, the first European convert, to the place of prayer and the Philippian gaoler to his knees before Paul and Silas is the same power today.

The power which built up the church in a pagan Roman Empire also built up a church of more than thirty million in Communist China and kept the church alive for three generations in Russia.

For three or four decades secular humanism has been the faith with most influence on European leadership. They claim that, since there are now so many different beliefs in all our countries, we must make our laws and practice conform to the view that every belief is equally valid. Yet this is a dogmatic, but precarious position which is unlikely to survive under pressure, since the major faiths in Europe, Christian and Jewish, Muslim and Sikh, all hold that they are uniquely true.

We Christians can afford to be tolerant of what we believe to be untrue. Our long experience shows that the Maker's Instructions which we hold in trust and which we try to explain to our own generation contain the divine wisdom which shows society how to live together in peace, and the truth we preach touches the divinely placed chords of conscience in the human heart, and gives us the conscience-driven urge to do what we ought to do.

In today's Europe all Christians are also citizens and all citizens are free to speak and responsible for deciding who shall govern us.

We Christians above all, ought to take this responsibility seriously, because government is ordained of God and it is he who has given us the responsibility. Now, as well as local government and national government, we as citizens are responsible at this critical time for the government of our continent.

Christians are also custodians of God's law by which all men and women should live and by which we will all be judged. We are not a sect whose private rules concern no one else.

Nor are we religious autocrats who can force society to obey laws which they do not wish to keep. We are in the same position as Moses who, having laid down the moral law that a marriage made two 'one flesh', still allowed divorce because, as Our Lord put it, of 'the hardness of your hearts'.

But Christians, relying on conscience and the ability of everyone to see what is good for others if not for themselves, 'accusing and excusing one another', should edge our neighbours as close as we can to a Christian social order.

It is a struggle, but it is not impossible, with God's help. He has told us to pray, 'Your will be done on earth as it is in heaven'. So we should pray and believe that our prayers will be answered.

Over the two thousand years since Christ's birth the mustard seed of the Christian faith has turned into a great tree, sheltering all kinds of fowls. It has leavened the lump of our society. It has brought Europe from paganism to faith, as we have fallen away, reformation and revivals have brought us back.

The Christian faith has helped to give Europe the scientific method, democracy and the rule of law, education, a respect for the dignity of women, the abolition of slavery and the freedom of labour to negotiate its terms of contract. The European declaration of human rights is wholly secular in presentation but wholly Christian in content. It is, in short, the cement which holds Europe together and we Christians are its custodians, not just for our generation but for the future.

2

Religious Liberties

Mike Morris

Christmas 1989 Chichester. The phone rings interrupting family celebrations on Christmas eve. A clear voice informs me the caller is speaking from Budapest. They run through some of the remarkable events taking place in Romania. Christmas moves onto the back burner and my focus becomes Romania and the evangelical Church there.

The speed of events as the former socialist bloc countries broke free from totalitarianism was staggering. Under the eyes of the world's press nascent democracies were born through extraordinary people movements. Maps need to be completely redrawn. A new age was dawning and hope was rising. A spirit of euphoria gripped the Western world; United States President, George Bush, declared the birth of a 'new world order'; things would never be the same again in this 'best of all possible worlds'!

Yet the cynicism (or realism) of Voltaire serves as a timely reminder to us all. The days of fraternity and freedom have been replaced by wars on the continent of Europe for the first time since the conflagration of 1939–45. National identity, accusation and counter accusation, the poison bottled up through years of tyrannical rule have all conspired to tarnish the early applause from a world that held its breath and cheered more from relief than conviction.

The problem we face is that we would like national and international relationships to be harmonious. The fact of national pride which expresses itself so often in bigotry is something we would like to disguise. Organisations such as the United Nations (UN) have our vote and yet have proved helpless on so many occasions simply because member nations refuse to accept an external mediator.

Whilst we might like to assume that the world is improving in respect of human rights and liberties, and even to seek to draw encouragement from the enhanced role which the UN now seems to be given, the facts confronting us speak for themselves. The globe is becoming less safe and an increasingly alien environment for vast numbers of people. Yesterday's heroes become today's tyrants; the oppressed so easily turn into the oppressors.

Returning briefly to Romania, a number of Christian agencies requested that the Evangelical Alliance of the United Kingdom (EAUK) should seek to co-ordinate an effective, joint response to the situation confronting the evangelical Church in the wake of Ceausescu's fall. This was effectively achieved with physical and spiritual supplies being provided.

Indeed, it stands as a model of good practice of all that can be achieved through effective communication and co-operation. Resources within the UK Church were targeted to specific needs identified by national leadership within Romania. Those resources, which would probably have been released anyway in response to the televised and very real crisis in Romania, were actually placed at the disposal of the evangelical leaders in the country.

The agencies fulfilled their mandate; the national evangelical Church in Romania was served in meeting the needs of the Romanian people, whether Christian or not; and the EAUK acted as the catalyst in facilitating an effective co-operative venture.

However, against this constructive backdrop, within weeks of the departure of Ceausescu, the Orthodox Church in the country began to seek to circumscribe the activities of the evangelicals.

Christ's Church, which had suffered together, was now in danger of inflicting damage upon itself. The potential difficulty continues and illustrates what has already been written, that apparent liberty all too often turns into licence for new oppression, discrimination and even persecution.

Combating religious liberty abuse

> Whilst we live in a time of spectacular, even miraculous, political and religious transformation, the Church world-wide suffers some of the worst persecution in its entire history. Communist oppressions may be seen to be crumbling but other governments that demand total allegiance oppress those who worship another king. There is continued discrimination and persecution in the Islamic world and under certain East Asian religions and also inter communal conflict within Christian areas. Secular pressure increases in resisting and denying religious freedom. In particular, evangelism is often subject to violent opposition.

So runs the opening paragraph of the introductory paper for the World Evangelical Fellowship Religious Liberty Commission (WEFRLC) summarising current trends. How realistic is the content of such a paragraph?

A brief overview of the global situation will suffice. The Lausanne Committee on World Evangelisation (LCOWE) prepared statistics on a vast range of subjects in preparation for its 'Lausanne II' conference in Manila in 1989. Amongst these statistics was the staggering figure that the Christian Church has seen 40,450,000 martyrs since A.D. 33. However, 26,625,000 have taken place between 1900–1990. Hence ninety years of the twentieth century have seen over 60% of all Christian martyrs in the history of the Church. If one really wants to grasp the rapidly increasing number of martyrs during this century, consider that just under 10,000,000 have lost their lives since 1950. This is a trend that cannot be ignored!

It is estimated that today 300,000 Christians are martyred annually; that is 25,000 every month. By the time we reach the year 2000 those figures will have risen to 500,000 per year; 41,000 per month.

The alarming fact is that as we search for increased levels of acceptance and tolerance in our high tech world we have to face the fact that it is actually becoming more repressive and violent than ever.

One final statistic. The number of martyrs as a percentage of all Christians across the Christian century is 0.49%. However, amongst Christian leaders, this percentage rises to 2.0%. Those who seek to establish and lead the Church become prime targets for those who want to circumscribe religious liberty for Christians.

Why is there religious intolerance?

At the local level

Historically there have always been conflicts at community level between different religious groups. Differences of cultural and religious practice have led to discrimination. A dominant group will often oppress a minority living alongside them. In a time of difficulty – socially, economically or environmentally – one group may use another as scapegoats.

Whilst identifiable historically and easily explained, as the globe shrinks in size and certain areas become increasingly destabilised through war, food insecurity, hostile environment and the like, people on the move will increasingly come into conflict with each other. Furthermore, with the apparent rise of militancy amongst traditional religions and less familiar contexts such as animal rights and the green movement, it is to be expected that more local conflicts will emerge.

The challenge to national and regional government will be to exercise justice and to be seen to be doing so even in the face of extreme pressure from religious or other pressure groups. Insofar as good government is maintained, the opportunity to dialogue between nations and to intercede on behalf of various groups will exist. Such government will also encourage good community relations within nations where different ethnic groups live cheek by jowl. Extreme statements or action produce swift polarisation amongst communities and make for a more volatile social environment. Good government works to avoid such polarisation and that provides the challenge for the next century's politicians who are currently cutting their teeth.

In the years ahead it will be a mighty test for the apparent commitment to deploy the UN as international peacekeeper. To the extent that national governments will actively make themselves accountable to such a world body such an experiment will work. However, will the nations of the world be content to have the major decisions made by the existing security council members? Alternatively will the minority of rich and powerful nations be prepared to consult and work in co-equal partnership with many of the nations from what is termed the two thirds world?

International nightmare or dream ticket to future peaceful co-existence, it remains the challenge for the world's leadership as the twentieth century draws to its close.

At a national level

Through history there have been five main reasons why governments oppress, discriminate against or persecute religious groups within their domains:

1. Political philosophy

This is most clearly illustrated by the centrally run systems known as communist in this century. Whilst change has affected eastern Europe, large tracts of Asia and parts of Africa remain under the sway of this particular governmental model.

The stories of suffering endured by Christians for years in the Soviet bloc are legendary. However, even as I write there continues to be extreme persecution of Christians across China. Although, by all accounts, the fastest growing Church in the world today, detention, torture and death are the consequences for many Christians.

Obviously any system of thought that so completely determines

31

the whole of life, as communism claims to do, will brook no competitor for people's affections. The Church could become a powerful rival in winning these affections. In such a scenario the will of the state might be challenged publicly and so must be ruthlessly crushed or replaced by a placid, government controlled alternative which appears to offer spiritual solace but in fact operates as a further tool of state control.

Such rigorous regulation of a people is not confined to a communist doctrine. In fact, vigilance must be maintained to resist the loss of civil liberties which down the centuries many have fought hard to gain. Freedom of religion is one of these hard won liberties and is guaranteed by article 18 of the UN Declaration of Human Rights and Fundamental Freedoms. This states:

> Everyone has the right to freedom of thought, conscience and religion; this right includes freedom to change his religion or belief, and freedom, either alone or in the community with others and in public or private, to manifest his religion or belief in teaching, practice, worship and observance.

It is hardly imaginable for many that the freedom enjoyed for so long within the UK could be removed and yet such freedoms must be maintained by the common consent and active support of the people to resist any attempted encroachment by the state. An incoming tide moves slowly but eventually covers the sands.

2 Dominant religion

With the increase of so called fundamentalism within religions generally and most commonly reported within Islam, there is an increasing likelihood of elected and unelected governments ruling exclusively in favour of, or subject to the principles of specific religious groups.

In this century this was most clearly illustrated by Nepal. The birthplace of Buddha, Nepal is, in fact, the world's only Hindu kingdom. For years the Christian community was intimidated at a local and national level. The intimidation gave rise to imprisonment and physical violence. There were stiff penalties for changing religion and terms of imprisonment for baptising converts to Christianity.

The concerted prayers and actions of the Christian Church around the world eventually led to the constitution being rewritten and even for the government to issue formal Christmas greetings to the Christian Church in December 1991.

Such action demanded the involvement of politicians and presentations to the UN. For such a co-ordinated action, groups such as the Jubilee Campaign played an essential role both in the UK and the USA.

We are reminded that where a religious group begins to dictate the legislation and the culture of a nation, then those not of the dominant faith group are subject to illegitimate penalties, illegitimate by the standards of human rights understanding even if legitimised within their own national context by effective legislation.

Again with the flight of people in this shrinking world to the comforts of religion, we must beware of an unacceptable influence being exerted over those in government to build on a religious base to the exclusion of all other faith communities. Freedom to choose and to practise one's religion are fundamental freedoms and themselves guarantors of future liberties.

3 Secular government

In most cases a separation of state and religion should act as a safeguard against an unhealthy influence of religious precepts over legislation and human rights. However, this does not guarantee that government is not subject to the well orchestrated demands of the majority within the national population.

Turkey is a secular state. Its population's religion is predominantly Muslim. The constitution and the law guarantee rights for all religious minorities to practise their religion; to gather for worship and witness about the content of their faith.

Unfortunately, the evangelical community found itself subject to discrimination. Congregations were detained, often without charge; individuals incarcerated, intimidated and at times beaten; Christian converts found themselves losing their jobs. The law courts constantly found in favour of the evangelicals and released them without charge when their cases were

33

eventually brought to a court of law. Such activity served as a major distinctive to the Christian Church in general and to those considering changing religion in particular.

At the invitation of the evangelical churches I travelled to Turkey on behalf of the EAUK to meet with national leaders. After investigating the situation and with legal assessment from one of the leading lawyers in the country, together we adopted a strategy of seeking to address the government over this unwelcome intrusion into the religious practice of the evangelical community.

Cutting a long, three year process short, EAUK arranged for Sir Fred Catherwood, MEP and a vice president of the European Parliament to travel to Turkey and meet with the then deputy Prime Minister and the Justice Minister. The Church, for its part, prayed and fasted.

The outcome was a promise to provide a letter of understanding for the evangelical community. As a result, where congregations had not been able to hire public meeting places, they were now permitted to do so and even purchase, should they be in a financial position to do so.

External involvement had helped to identify the lack of consistency in a secular government discriminating against a national, religious minority. a commitment to continue in close association with that evangelical minority means that the current conditions can at all times be effectively monitored. The outworking can also be encouraged for the whole of Turkey which at present is not the case in practice.

Vigilance and effective political action is required in all such secular states. Life is continually moving; ideas change; social structures are subject to re-shaping; and hence the position of the Church is itself subject to review and perceived from different angles. What once served admirably may not be effective today. The same goes for tomorrow.

4 Conscience

In 1988 Jubilee Campaign reported on the case of Charles Bester. A white South African of 18 years he refused to serve in the South African Defence Force (SADF) as the law had demanded. The only exclusion was for conscientious objectors, which Bester claimed he was not.

His stance was that as a Christian he felt unable to serve in the SADF because it would mean confronting Black communities from the back of a combo, dressed in full riot gear and carrying a gun. Bester felt that for a nation whose future lay in the hands of the Black majority, it was not likely to enhance harmonious relations if he and countless other men his age engaged in meeting the Black community in this way. He took this stand quoting the Christian convictions arrived at from the study of Scripture.

The only option left open to the courts was to sentence him to imprisonment which they did for the statutory requirement of six years.

Obviously, many Christians across South Africa disagreed with Bester's stand. However, he felt on the basis of Christian conscience, informed through the study of the Bible and through prayer, together with consultation with Christian friends, this was the course he must adopt.

There are times when even in what might be deemed open societies operating on democratic principles, Christian conscience demands a course of action which has clear consequences. Scripture is clear about the need for minds that are transformed rather than conformed and the Church cannot simply allow itself the luxury of assuming that democracy is synonymous with godly government.

As the Church seriously applies Scriptural truth to the society in which it lives, there is increasing demand to communicate with the decision takers and at times, challenge their assumptions. Increasingly, as the worldview operating within a society develops, without reference to Biblical foundations, the points of conflict and hence challenge will increase. It will be the responsibility of the Church to identify the points of conflict and present the challenge. This is a major area of testing for the new found unity amongst evangelicals and will be a protection against such unity becoming reduced down to a basic minimum.

5 Tyranny

Finally, where unrestrained power operates, the Church suffers. Those who live as tyrants do not want to have their authority challenged nor their subjects conscientised. Whether it be Nero in Rome or Amin in Uganda, the organs of state are merely taken over and ruthlessly exploited to maintain and advance personal power. At all times it is the duty of the Church to decry such abuse of power.

As a teenager I well remember meeting Archbishop Janani Luwum of Uganda. His testimony of life in Uganda and prediction of his own murder, left a deep impression upon me and enabled me as a young Christian to begin to see how one's ideals could be effectively integrated into a life of Christian service.

I trust that we may as a result of giving ourselves wholeheartedly to such service, which is after all simply obeying God in the macro as well as the micro of our personal walk, we might see the demise of such tyrannies and increased support for those Christians and others who suffer so acutely under them.

Towards 2000 and beyond

As we race towards the year 2000, the whole area of human rights and religious liberty confronts us. The way in which such issues are handled will be a measure of the humanity we have. Our Christian calling which knows no geographical boundaries demands that we involve ourselves on behalf of the worldwide family.

In 1992 at its general assembly in Manila, Philippines, the World Evangelical Fellowship approved the establishment of a Religious Liberty Commission. In recognition of the difficulties facing so many believers worldwide, it was felt essential that the worldwide evangelical communities be kept informed and motivated to action, as appropriate.

The so called 'global village' requires that accurate information is exchanged swiftly and efficiently. Relationships need to be established with bodies such as the UN and other international and regional bodies in order that representation can be made and action encouraged. In a world where information is increasingly identified with power, it is again essential that information is processed and co-ordinated so that the most appropriate reporting and strategies can take place.

Many are the human rights guides that fill our bookshelves,

yet there is no major analysis of the state of religious liberty around the globe. In order to monitor the state of religion worldwide, such an analysis must be undertaken. Criteria need to be established by which we can honestly quantify the state of religious liberty. In this way the condition in the country will be made known to all.

Legal networks must be set up to enable communities and individuals to gain access to appropriate legal representation. A working knowledge of the legal codes and constitutional arrangements in the countries of the world also needs to be provided and presented to legal scholars and practitioners for considered opinion.

Evangelical communities at both National and Regional levels must be encouraged and enabled to argue on their own behalf for religious liberty and engage in dialogue with government where appropriate.

In order to secure religious liberties into the next century these will be the means. Drawing from the ongoing and tireless efforts of a host of existing organisations, the Religious Liberty Commission provides an effective mechanism for responding to requests from national and regional church leadership and a forum for collating the essential information gathering of such organisations.

One final word for those displaced people who have no country of their own: I speak of the refugees. By the end of 1992 there will be 20 million refugees in the world and half of these will be children. The UNHCR states that 80% are from the two thirds world. The rise of refugees has been from a figure of 1 million in 1951, rising to 8 million in 1981 to the staggering figures today.

As governments move to seal borders, what is the outcome for the rising tide of the world's wanderers? Has the Church anything to say for such sojourners? Or will she remain silent? Plans to ease the problems of religious liberty are under way. But a further challenge remains with regard to the refugees.

The next century will continue to produce issues demanding an international response orchestrated from a local level and an opportunity for the Church to be in the vanguard rather than the rear-guard.

These words summarise some of the virtues expected of the Christian. Lucian satirising the Christian practice, indicates how effectively they support each other when, in writing of the imprisonment of Proteus Peregrinus, he says:

> (the Christians) left no stone unturned in their endeavour to procure his release. When this proved impossible, they looked after his wants in all other matters with untiring solicitude and devotion. From earliest dawn old women and orphan children might be seen waiting about the prison doors; whilst the officers of the Church, by bribing the jailors, were able to spend the night inside with him. Meals were brought in, and they went through their sacred formulas.

This reflected observable Christian practice around AD 115. Such practice is challenging to the Church today. It is our responsibility to seek to raise our voice for those who, being silenced, have no voice of their own. As Gerald Coates is fond of saying:

> 'You can't change everyone's world everywhere, but you can change somebody's world somewhere!'

With religious liberty being challenged all over the world, the word to the Church is vigilance. When so many millions of God's image bearers are displaced and categorised as refugees, it is time for God's Church to respond with active compassion recognising that behind every statistic lies a human tragedy.

Making a difference

The writer to the Hebrews wrote, amongst final exhortations:

> Keep on loving each other as brothers. Do not forget to entertain strangers, for by so doing some people have entertained angels without knowing it. Remember those in prison as if you were their fellow prisoners,

and those who are ill treated as if you yourselves were
suffering. (Hebrews 13:1–3)

How can this be done?

Be informed. Without regular and accurate information,
nothing can be achieved. There are many organisations who can
provide that information and a letter to the International
Administrator at the Evangelical Alliance, Whitefield House, 186
Kennington Park Road, London SE11 4BT, will assure you a
list of member organisations of the Religious Liberty Coalition.

You could focus on one part of the world or take responsibility
for particular cases around the globe. It also provides an effective
means of learning about the Church worldwide and provides a
significant way of building fellowship links with brothers and
sisters worldwide.

Be prayerful. It is essential to pray for situations. There is
no doubt that the level of prayer focused on what was Eastern
Europe played a significant part in both the political changes
and the growth of the Church under oppressive regimes. One
trusts as much prayer is being invested in the new political
structures as they emerge.

With information we can pray personally; we can ensure the
church prayer meeting is guided to intercede on behalf of the
suffering Church; we can also request time to make short
presentations into the main church worship meetings. So often
praying has taken a low profile in such gatherings yet positively
led, the church family can be blessed and become a blessing.

Be active. The information you sign up will, from time to
time, require specific action. Letters directed to an appropriate
ambassador or government minister might be necessary.
Amnesty International (AI), who have led the field in
campaigning on human rights in general and prisoners of
conscience in particular, have time and time again demonstrated
the importance of letters in relieving the sufferings of imprisoned
individuals.

Such action is best orchestrated by an existing agency in touch
with national and regional Church leadership. Taking action
without such advice can seriously jeopardise the life of the
Christian community.

Opportunities also abound in certain situations to travel and visit the Church in another nation and culture. This is tremendously encouraging. Just to utilise holiday time and the availability of travel can increase our understanding of the Church overseas, but also greatly hearten the local believers. However, the idea is to visit and enjoy fellowship, not to preach, influence another congregation or find stories to relate back home, enhancing the position of the story-teller at the visited's expense. The trauma of Romania and other nations following the fall of the Berlin Wall is a stern reminder to us all of the worst aspects of so called Christian solidarity.

Finally with so many refugees on the move, is your Church prepared to receive a 'bona fide' asylum seeker? There is such an amount of paperwork in processing a request for asylum that the individual needs a stable base, providing him with board, lodging and fellowship. Often in a strange culture the refugee needs stability in order to come to terms with the current situation and also the stress of the very process of applying for asylum. As Churches we should be able to provide such hospitality to strangers.

Such action may seem very little but when the Lebanese Church leaders requested that the EAUK invite its membership to send letters and cards of general encouragement, spirits were lifted in underground shelters all over Beirut. Encouragement that renewed the ability of the Church, suffering in that hideous situation, to continue to be faithful through trying circumstances and emerge victorious.

> If one part suffers, every part suffers with it; if one part
> is honoured, every part rejoices with it (1 Corinthians
> 12:26).

So it is with the worldwide body of Christ and we are all members of it, called to play our part to great effect.

3

Domestic Politics

Martyn Eden

Who cares?

Politics without some sort of faith is impossible but, paradoxically, when faith and politics are mixed they can produce a heady, if not explosive, brew. The examples of Islamic fundamentalism in Iran or the religion-based politics of Northern Ireland spring quickly to mind. For that reason, even such politicians as Lord Hailsham, who profess a Christian faith, advocate keeping the two well apart.[1] For much of this century, support for this segregation has come from those evangelicals who, for a variety of reasons, have seen political involvement as a distraction from Biblical priorities and best left to others. In light of this, a chapter on political trends in this book may require some justification. Nevertheless, there are very good reasons for its inclusion.

At the time of writing there are three Bills before Parliament which are arousing varying degrees of agitation and activity amongst evangelicals. These relate to Sunday trading, euthanasia and the creation of a national lottery. On top of these, there are other issues – racism, unemployment, homelessness and the extreme poverty and famine in developing nations – which have also been stimulating Biblical reflection and practical initiatives amongst evangelicals. At a more general level, there is growing concern amongst Christian housing associations and voluntary societies working with people who are disadvantaged, that they are less and less acceptable to secular public bodies because of their faith basis.

In this context, the sacred-secular divide is no longer a credible option, even if it were Biblically defensible, which is itself highly debatable. A realistic appraisal of political trends is essential for evangelicals at three levels – for Christian leaders and activists who interact with the political system, for intercessors and prayer ministries, and for all Christian citizens who wish to honour Jesus as Lord in every dimension of life.

What trends?

However, identifying these trends is notoriously difficult and many an attempt has proved disastrously wrong. This is partly because the very closeness to current events which gives us our factual knowledge also impedes our efforts to put them into the historical perspective required to identify patterns and trends. If this familiarity is also loaded with partisan sentiments, our judgement is further clouded.

Time scale is another complicating factor. When Harold Wilson observed that a week is a long time in politics, he was referring to the short-term nature of much of British politics. This week's cause célèbre is next week's history. British voters, typically, have short political memories. The furthest horizon for most politicians is the next election and so much of the detail is thought about in relation to the annual budget cycle and the parliamentary session. Discerning long-term trends in this context is generally the work of academics rather than practitioners.

Even for the academics, the hardest challenge in trend spotting is to project them forward into the future. What new factors could come into play and alter the trend? A war, a natural disaster or a sudden substantial rise in fuel prices could all render the best laid plans irrelevant. In the last few years, the speed of the disintegration of the USSR and the Warsaw Pact surprised many observers and played havoc with our trend projections.

On top of this, governments are confronted with more and more apparently insoluble problems. For example, we do not yet know when scientists will find a cure for AIDS or how far it will spread into the heterosexual population. So, we cannot have an accurate idea of the likely effects of AIDS on demographic trends. Wherever there are such imponderable factors, it is easier to see where we have come from than where we are going, yet it is the latter which we really want to know in order to plan or act appropriately.

Readers will be aware already that the potential scope of this chapter far exceeds the scale of this book. Notwithstanding cuts in government activity in the last decade, the government still touches the citizen's life at most steps from the cradle to the grave. It is only possible in this brief essay to take account of a few aspects of contemporary political trends, with apologies to those who think the wrong ones have been selected.

Government trends

A good place to start discerning political trends is in the Government's manifesto. The April 1992 Election was a contest between alternative programmes for the direction of the nation over the next 4–5 years and the people who would be implementing them. Barring the direst crises, the resulting overall majority of twenty-one should be sufficient to sustain the Conservatives in office, even if they lose the occasional by-election. Provided they retain the support of their members in the House of Commons, they are constitutionally free to implement their manifesto. If they are frustrated in this, it will be because of factors they have not taken into account, for whatever reason, and most likely because of economic factors. The British economy depends heavily on international trade and is therefore open to the impact of world commodity price movements and exchange rate fluctuations. Decisions made in the financial centres of Europe, Japan and the USA can and do influence our economy in ways beyond the control of the British Government. Even so, government has more to say about political trends than anyone else.

John Major summed up his party's 1992 manifesto in the language of responsible individualism. 'You, and not the Government, should be in charge of your life.'[2] His vision for Britain in the 90s is one in which the Government's role is limited so that individual opportunity, choice, ownership and responsibility can be maximised. Price stability is the key economic goal and was to have been achieved through public expenditure constraint and membership of the European Exchange Rate Mechanism (ERM). The fragility of this policy (and the difficulty of trend discerning) was demonstrated when the second strand of the policy foundered less than six months after the election. Doubts about the health of the British economy, together with high German interest rates, pushed the Pound's exchange rate below its ERM permitted minimum, forcing the Government to withdraw Sterling from membership.

Unquestionably, the rate at which the British economy pulls out of recession in 1992-3 and grows thereafter, will be the most important factor determining whether or not the Government's vision for Britain is realised. The early signs will give them little encouragement. The relatively high rate of economic growth achieved in the 80s involved a high level of personal consumption financed from credit. When interest rates rose and the level of unemployment with them, a lot of people found themselves embarrassed by debt. The record number of home repossessions by building societies is one sad piece of evidence. They will not be in a hurry to repeat that experience. Because the Government is also holding down public expenditure in its fight against inflation, demand will rise only very sluggishly, which will keep unemployment at wastefully high levels well into the decade. It will also inhibit the Government's intention to further reduce the rates of personal income tax.

Our membership of the European Union is another key element of the Government strategy which will influence political trends in the 90s. Although there are minorities in both the Conservative and Labour parties opposed to the 'European dream', our trade patterns make continuing membership of the community commercially unavoidable. However, amongst the core EC nations – France, Germany, Belgium, The Netherlands, Italy and Luxemburg – trade and economics are not primarily what the community is about. For them it is about reconciliation and building the closer social ties that will prevent a repeat of the devastating experience of two world wars in the lifetime of one generation. This mismatch in motives and all that follows from it, seems destined to keep Europe as a thorny issue on our political agenda, both domestically and in our community relations, for years to come. Slow economic growth and a relatively weak Pound can only exacerbate this.

The value which the Conservatives place on responsible individualism will continue to find expression in the privatisation of the nationalised industries. The National Coal Board and British Rail are next in line but neither will be as easy to sell off as were the electricity, telecommunications and water industries. More significant for most of us will be what happens to the health and caring services. Here the Government is seeking to reap what they see as the benefits of market discipline, without privatisation per se. In the National Health Service, hospitals are being encouraged to opt out of the bureaucratic model and to compete in terms of the quality of service they offer. Patients are notionally free to shop around, to obtain the service they rquire. Scepticism about this approach is rooted in a suspicion that those in greatest need are often least able to exercise consumer choice, even assuming that they are accurately informed about the options open to them.

A parallel strategy is being applied to the personal social services. Traditional caring institutions are being closed and the emphasis being switched to care in the community. Local Authorities are responsible for co-ordinating service provision but not necessarily for providing care. Services will be put out to tender and contracts awarded to the agencies with the best bids, within prescribed standards. There is widespread agreement that community care has a place in any personal social services strategy, provided there is adequate funding and effective quality control. Doubts about likely levels of funding, which have their roots in the anticipated slow rate of economic growth in the 90s, suggest that the Government's aspirations will not be achieved. The policy also assumes that families will take on greater responsibility for the care of their more dependent members. However, current trends in family life raise questions as to the capacity of many families to play the part intended for them. Whilst the commitment to the family and to personal responsibility are welcome from a Christian standpoint, we must not ignore the down side of human nature and the possibility that the quality of life for some will become unacceptably poor as they are neglected in uncaring communities. The challenge for Churches is obvious.

These trends must be set against the background of Government intentions with regard to personal wealth and ownership. As economic circumstances permit, they aim to further reduce the basic rate of income tax towards 20p. Their goal is to leave more spending power and scope for choice in the hands of wage earners. They see this as a means of encouraging wider home and share ownership. The threshold for the inheritance tax is also to be raised. Obviously, these measures are all about nurturing a culture conducive to the Conservative's capitalist values. However, they carry with them the potential to create or exacerbate a variety of problems which are likely to be the key issues in the 1996–7 General Election.

First, lower rates of income tax mean an increased dependence upon other taxes, especially Value Added Tax. Inevitably this raises questions of fairness since VAT is a regressive tax. Secondly, any increase in private affluence must be equated with increased public squalor as services are constrained by budgetary requirements. This might be avoided in a period of vigorous economic growth but the prospects for this have already been described as poor. Moreover, the affluence of those in well paid jobs will not be shared by those who, for a whole variety of reasons, are unemployed. The strategy is also distressing to those involved in the ecological debate. The magnitude of the problems facing our society and, indeed, the whole planet, require collective decisions tht do not accord with the Government's emphasis on the individual.

There is obviously a great deal more to Government policy than the few points summarised here. The selection has had only one consideration in mind: in which direction is the Government trying to steer the nation? What sort of society do they want Britain to be? The answer is summed up in their slogan, 'responsible individualism'. To the extent that this reflects one element of God's creation pattern, evangelicals will welcome it but insofar as it overlooks others, we will be sceptical. The Biblical worldview places a lot of value on individuals, made as we are in God's image, but we are not autonomous beings, to do as we please, because we are accountable to our Creator. Moreover, the Bible also makes clear that we are created to be inter-dependent with one another. The same theme is taken up in the New Testament. God's people are saved into community, to serve others. Partisanship apart, it has to be said that insofar as the present Government's vision for Britain lacks these perspectives, it is flawed and its architects will be frustrated in their endeavours.

Alternative approaches

Of course, if there is a change of Government in the second half of the decade, then there are bound to be changes of direction. The nature of these changes will depend on what happens within and between the opposition parties over the next four years, as well as the mix of domestic and international issues confronting us then. Even so, some things are foreseeable. The Labour Party, alone or in partnership with the Liberal Democrats, will surely be less individualistic and more interventionist in its basic philosophy. Although the Labour Party has shed some of its traditional socialist ideology, it remains an egalitarian party with a moral imperative to combat poverty and to challenge privilege. Circumstances permitting, a Labour challenge would substantially increase public expenditure to stimulate investment in industry, increase the availability of affordable homes and to expand Government activity across the social welfare programmes.

The real contrast with the Conservatives is best illustrated by this statement from the 1992 Labour manifesto. 'For liberty to have real meaning the standards for community provision must be high and access to that provision must be wide'.

Regardless of who is in office, some items on the political agenda will remain the same. Indeed, some would say that these items are more significant than the domestic issues that have been addressed so far. The physical state of the planet will continue to deteriorate until bold international initiatives are taken to arrest pollution and conserve natural resources for future generations. The Green agenda is closely linked with the needs of developing nations. Their indebtedness to the rich, developed countries helps to perpetuate dehumanising levels of poverty and sometimes drives them to ecologically disastrous exploitation of their natural resources. On the world stage, a number of familiar scenarios will continue to unfold in Eastern Europe, Southern Africa and the Middle East. Closer to home, the expansion of the EC, its democratic accountability and a succession of minor community crises will compete for media attention.

Flaws in the system

It is also highly probable that parts of the political system itself will come under increasing pressure for reform. At the time of writing, what are sometimes called the dignified parts of the constitution are under scrutiny – especially the monarchy. Controversy surrounding the younger members of the Queen's family have been commercially exploited by the tabloids for some time but when the chairman of the Conservative backbenchers' 1922 committee publicly advocates that the Queen should pay tax and the civil list should be severely pruned, the issue has become serious. It is unlikely that the monarchy will be abolished but some genuine adjustments in the Civil List, in personal lifestyles and in relationships with the media will be needed if the royal family is to recover the respect and affection which it enjoyed ten years ago.

The British electoral system has long been subject to criticism, particularly from the minority parties which suffer from its distorting effects. The two largest parties have always favoured the present 'first past the post' system because it usually produces clear majorities and because it has favoured their interests. That was considered acceptable whilst there was a reasonable frequency of alternation between them. Were the Labour Party to lose a fifth successive election, it is highly likely to support the calls for reform which are already heard amongst some of its members. Moreover, there are other pressures for electoral reform which are likely to intensify in the 1990s. If proportional representation were to be introduced for elections to the European Parliament, or for Scottish, Welsh and Ulster Assemblies, this could easily be a thin end of the wedge so far as Westminster elections are concerned.

A third institution that is likely to be the subject of debate in the 90s is Local Government. When the modern pattern of representative democracy was thought out in the last century, local councils were seen not only as the provider of services best organised locally, but also as a vehicle for democratic education and apprenticeship. The issues were more likely to be intelligible, the politicians were more accessible and the sense of immediacy aroused interest even in relatively mundane matters. A hundred years on, life is more complex and some of those activities are now better organised nationally. The scope for local autonomy has been eroded over a long period but never more deliberately than in the 1980s.

Some citizens now have the appearance of an increased involvement and responsibility, as with the local management of schools, but the reality is very different. Responsibility for a particular school is different in kind as well as scale from the overall responsibility for a community's schools, such as local education authorities used to have. The real political control of schools is gradually being transferred to central Government. The effect is to make the government process more remote from citizens and as this happens in other areas too, our democratic political culture is being changed. As the divide between THEM and US is widened, the levels of alienation felt by citizens will increase. At the same time, local community loyalties are being undermined. The long-term consequence could be to make Britain a harder country to govern so this is a trend to be watched and challenged. Certainly the loss of community experienced in many urban areas will not help the development of community care policies.

Underlying all these trends is the drift to relativism in ethics and behaviour. We saw this in the further liberalisation of the abortion legislation in the last decade. In the 90s, it is manifested in the growing pressure for the legalisation of euthanasia. It will also be increasingly difficult for faith-based projects to obtain public funds for caring initiatives unless they are willing to compromise in a variety of ways. A 'Christian only' staffing policy is likely to be considered unacceptable in a pluralist society. Christian groups who refuse to employ practising homosexuals will be dismissed as homophobic. Even prayer before meetings could be grounds for disqualification. There are already examples of each of these pressures: the trend will be towards their proliferation.

Bad news or what?

This scenario may seem very negative but that is not the intention. As we recognised at the outset, for much of the twentieth century evangelicals have tended to stay outside politics. True, over the last twenty years there has been a gradual re-engagement with social issues and caring initiatives but comparatively few evangelicals have been brave enough to enter the political arena. Sadly, it was whilst the Christian salt and light was understrength that the relativist rot set in. The challenge now is to try to arrest and even reverse the drift by starting a new political trend of our own.

Is this realistic? How do we go about it? In all but the final resort, assessments of realism depend on one's starting point. Nothing will seem realistic to those who do not want to face up to the challenge but others may be encouraged to be more openminded by three considerations. First Jesus' salt and light metaphors must surely mean that if we penetrate society in the same way that salt was rubbed into meat to preserve it, we can make a difference. The metaphor is not grounds for evangelical triumphalism but it does offer a basis for some optimism. This is reinforced, secondly, by the evidence of contemporary sociology. American sociologist, Robert Bellah suggests, on the basis of his research, that if at least 2% of the nation are committed to changing it, they have a better than even prospect of doing so. Thirdly, this proposition is genuinely consistent with the evidence of nineteenth century British history. Evangelicals such as Wilberforce and Hannah Moore, Shaftesbury and Booth, were salt and light in their time and they did make a difference. So how could we emulate them today?

There is probably no single recipe but there are some key ingredients. The most crucial are people with commitment, an appropriate, live spirituality and the adoption of responsible, professional methods. The prior need for believers committed to the task is obvious. There are many forms and levels of political involvement but they all call for a measure of commitment. The active Christian citizen takes time to keep up with current affairs, to acquire at least a basic grasp of the major issues and to pray and reflect Biblically on them. The party or issue-group activists give even more time to meetings and to campaigning whilst the office holders have both to stand for election and, if successful, to fulfil the duties of office. These demands usually come on top of family, church and occupational commitment so the depth of commitment has to be sacrificial. Moreover, the sort of changes that are called for in Britain will not come easily or quickly so the duration of commitment is also important. The person who moves like a butterfly from issue to issue according to what is in vogue at the moment, is no help at all. Equally crucial is the direction of commitment. Politics can be a huge ego trip so if our goal is not to glorify God and to manifest His kingly rule then we would be better advised to leave well alone.

Realism about politics tells us the importance of an appropriate, live spirituality. Power and proximity to those who wield it can be very seductive. It is not uncommon for people to enter the political arena with strong ideals and then gradually to sacrifice them to achieve acceptance and influence. Compromise is unavoidable in democratic politics but if we compromise our basic Christian values just to rub shoulders with the powerful, how can we make a difference? 'If the salt loses its saltiness, it is good for nothing'. So realism about human nature and especially our own is essential. So too is realism about our capacities in relation to the size and nature of the task. We are not going to eliminate sin or to consummate God's Kingdom by our efforts. Only Christ can do that, when He returns. Again, we do not have all the answers or a monopoly of wisdom: only He has these. Thus realism teaches us the need to stay close to Him and to operate in His strength and under His guidance. To be effective salt in our political system requires a mature prayer life and a deep familiarity with, and understanding of God's word. It probably means being in fellowship with Christians who will support you when the going is tough and challenge you when they think you need challenging. The unavoidable conclusion is that the more demanding levels of political involvements should only be tackled by Christians with a clear sense of calling which is confirmed by the Church fellowship, which then commits itself to support their sister or brother who has been called. Not many churches have begun to think in such terms, yet.

Counter trends

Given such highly committed and mature Christians, how will they set about influencing political trends? Inevitably, the answer must be tentative because the evidence so far is limited. A characteristic of much evangelical political effort in the recent past has been its reactive nature. A policy is announced or a Bill is presented to Parliament and a protest is gradually organised. The result is that evangelicals are too frequently seen as 'anti' everything. This is a psychologically weak basis from which to campaign and it gives evangelicals a poor image. Moreover, the initiative is usually with the other side. Of course there have been instances such as the 1986 Shops Bill, when it was possible to seize the initiative but there have been others, such as the Human Fertilisation and Embryology Bill, when we failed with tragic consequences for some. Nineteenth century evangelicals were regularly proactive in the political arena to very good effect and the more that we can follow their example, the more impact we are likely to have.

However, realists will object that evangelicals are not strong enough to seize the political initiative, acting on our own. That is generally true. The campaign to Keep Sunday Special is a good example. Humanly speaking, the churches alone could not have defeated the Government in 1986, nor sustain the subsequent Sunday Campaign at the level at which it has operated. The contributions of many secular organisations have been important. This has sometimes meant compromise on points of detail but never of principle. The alternative would have been defeat and total deregulation in 1986. We have to recognise that on many issues there will be non-Christians who share specific political goals with us. Feminist groups share our opposition to pornography. Muslims are as much against secularisation as we are. Our concern to protect family values is shared by many Conservatives and our commitment to racial justice is shared by many on the left. In other respects, we may have difficulties working with those who do not share our worldview but this need not prevent co-belligerence on matters about which we agree and it could make all the difference between success or failure.

A third step towards influencing political trends involves improving the flow of reliable political intelligence, analysis and evaluation. Too much contemporary evangelical discussion and prayer about politics seems to be based on ill-informed comment and pious attitudes. The new Parliamentary Briefing Service for Churches, which is being discussed as this book goes to print, would help to correct this weakness. The Jubilee Policy Analysis Group also has an important role to play, just as soon as more evangelicals wake up to the value of the group's work and are prepared to commission research. Biblical reflection on the issues of the day, after the model of John Stott's *Issues Facing Christians Today*, is also imperative if we are to do more than echo the world. The Institute for Contemporary Christianity is a central resource for this, offering both courses and study packs for use at home. It is not as though the means are not available; if only more evangelicals would make use of them.

Of course, the study is not an end in itself but a basis for action. Once again, there is no shortage of opportunities for those who feel called to become actively involved. There are Christian groups within each of the major political parties. The Movement for Christian Democracy is not yet a party but it does have policy groups on economic issues, education, foreign affairs, people with disabilities and the contributions of elderly people to our society.

Care Campaigns is well organised at the local constituency level and addresses issues such as abortion, euthanasia and pornography. It also incorporates the go-ahead Christians in Education team. In addition, there are many other groups, both evangelical and more broadly based, such as the Churches National Housing Coalition, Church Action on Poverty and the Christian Ecology Link.

Identifying political trends is far from a precise science. An examination of the present government's intentions, taken together with the effects of underlying social currents, give us some clues as to where Britain is heading. If evangelicals do not find these clues entirely to our liking, we have very few grounds for complaining because our influence as salt and light was missing when it was needed most. The argument of this chapter has been that it is still not too late to make amends and to influence political trends if we have will and a calling to do so. Who has that calling?

Notes

1 Hailsham in M. Alison and D. Edwards, *Christianity and Conservatism* (Hodder and Stoughton, London, 1990).
2 *The Conservative Manifesto 1992*.

4

Family

Joan King

There was the sound of a heavy thud, followed by a rattle and another thud. Jenny stirred. 'What was that?' she asked.

'The postman,' replied Graham. 'Sounds like there's a lot of mail today. Happy anniversary, luv.'

Jenny smiled as she threw on her dressing gown. 'Happy anniversary,' she replied. 'Imagine! Fifty years and it seems like yesterday.'

The phone rang. It was some of the grandchildren. 'Congratulations' they sang. 'See you later at the party.'

Still in their dressing gowns, and with a mug of tea each, Jenny and Graham opened the mail. 'This one is from Ruth and there's a letter . . . it's good to read her news.'

As Jenny and Graham read their cards, memories came flooding back. They remembered their hopes and dreams as they set out on their marriage, as well as some of the struggles, pains and joys of their fifty years together. The greetings they received reminded them of people who had crossed and enriched their path – friends, neighbours and family. They talked of significant places – their various homes and the different churches to which they had belonged. All of these contributed to a kaleidoscope of memories as they reflected together on this, their golden wedding day.

Like many couples of their generation Graham and Jenny were married during World War II at a time of national and international insecurity. Life was a struggle at first but they had youth on their side and hoped that a better world would result in which they might raise children. Together Graham and Jenny, and others like them, are evidence that marriage can last. It can be a nurturing and enriching experience but it may never be easy. At no other time in history have so many couples celebrated golden or diamond weddings. That is good news at a time when the demise of the family is what is often communicated by the media, and others.

Perhaps it is because change makes more dramatic news than continuity that it seems to attract the most attention leaving us with the impression that there was a golden age of family. The emphasis today is that there is a decline in family life and values. Is this really so?

When Jenny and Graham were young they belonged to large, extended families. Graham was the youngest of seven. As a child he shared a double bed with three brothers. They slept top to tail like sardines in a can. The whole family shared a three-bedroomed cottage in which the kitchen was the centre of warmth and communication. It was here that a fire was always alight and where the tin bath was used each week.

As Graham received the greetings of his surviving brothers and sisters on this anniversary he remembered his childhood home with affection. Both his parents worked long, gruelling days, his father being in paid employment and his mother unpaid but employed in home-making with none of the conveniences which make light work of it today. When his older sisters went to work 'in service', lodgers took their room and became part of the family for whom mother cared. There had been hard times financially and materially but always love and affection were present. Relatives and friends from the community were on hand to help out. The door of their house was never locked. People came and went. They belonged to a community in which the church brought people together. He met Jenny through the church.

Graham smiled reflectively. 'What are you thinking about?' teased Jenny. 'The good old days! I was wondering how good they were. Remember our wedding reception and how everyone saved food coupons so that we could have a good spread?'

'That ham salad was the best I've ever tasted – perhaps because all the family and neighbours gave and worked to make it possible. It was a real community effort. Things are different today.'

'Well,' replied Graham, 'families are much smaller and more private. Somehow they seem to be like little islands which are meant to be self-sufficient.'

'That's true,' agreed Jenny. 'Harry told me that he and Elizabeth have been living in their flat in the city for three months and they still have not met the neighbours on their landing. It'll be hard for Elizabeth when the baby's born.'

'Imagine! Our first great-grandchild! We'll be a four-generation family. I hope their church will give Elizabeth and Harry the support they'll need as young parents. They're a long way from the rest of us.'

Thinking of a great-grandchild Jenny's thoughts turned to the births of her three children. She and Graham were proud of them all. They had chosen to have three children rather than seven like Graham's parents or five like her own. Their generation may have been brought up in 'a golden age' but there was a lot that was not golden about it. Her own mother had died in childbirth when she was five. She'd been brought up by her older sisters supported by aunts and uncles living locally, while her father worked to provide. When not at work he laboured in the garden producing vegetables and caring for the chickens that ensured that the family had wholesome food to eat. Dad seemed a distant person. She knew he loved her but he did not express his feelings easily.

Sometimes when Jenny read the news about children and one-parent families in the 1990s she thought about life in her family headed by a widowed father. Hers was not the only family like that either. There were families who had lost a parent through industrial injury, alcohol and World War 1. It seemed to her that one-parent families were not a new phenomenon but today the reasons were different ie because of divorce, separation or choice. In her day, however, one-parent families had other kinfolk nearby and were part of the community. There were more adults involved in the lives of the children.

Jenny's perceptions were accurate. About one-third of lone-parent families result from divorce and the rate of divorce is increasing rapidly. The figures look like this. Of marriages taking place in:

1951   Ten per cent ended in divorce by twenty-five years
1971   Ten per cent ended in divorce by six years
1981   Ten per cent ended in divorce by four-and-a-half years

The 1991 figures are not available at the time of writing but we do know that Britain is now at the top of the league for divorce in Europe. It seems that many marriages are lasting for shorter periods though the idea of marriage remains popular. These statistics may be alarming but they need to be seen within the context of a society in which most people's marriages last a life-time. Most people marry, have children and make the necessary adjustments at each stage of their family life to enable them to continue living in committed relationship.

The reasons why couples divorce vary but recent research would suggest that people have very high expectations of the relationship, perhaps too high to make it workable. They expect their marriage relationship to meet all emotional, psychological and economic needs with little support from family, friends, church or the wider community. In addition marriages are expected to last longer because of the increased longevity of life. There are more life adjustments to make and often communication patterns established early in marriage are not developed enough to enable communication at crisis points in the relationship. There is a challenge here for the Christian churches to which the majority of couples still come for marriage. The wedding day is only the beginning for the church. How does it continue to support and nurture married couples? No marriage is perfect. Relationships are fragile. They need support throughout life.

The door bell rang. 'I'll go,' said Graham. He was excited today. 'Who is it?' called Jenny.

It was Interflora with a huge arrangement of yellow and white flowers. 'How beautiful,' whispered Jenny as Graham handed her the card. 'They are from Fiona and the boys.' Fiona was their middle child and the divorced one. She had married in the late sixties, in the days of miniskirts and Beatles shortly after leaving teacher training college. Her husband was young and ambitious. Graham and Jenny had been so proud of them. They were going to have a good life having had the tertiary education which was not available to their parents. The grandchildren were born in the mid 70s and Fiona dedicated herself to them while her husband concentrated on his job and promotion prospects. Fiona became more involved with the local church and grew as a Christian. The boys were involved too but her husband gradually showed less interest. It was as if communication ceased between them. Then there was the dreadful day when Fiona informed her parents that after twelve years of marriage she and her husband were divorcing.

Jenny and Graham had been shattered. They determined to support their daughter no matter what. It had been hard at first, especially among their Christian friends, but they knew that they did not want Fiona to live in misery. In their day there were plenty of couples who stayed together for economic reasons and the women were trapped by lack of education, income, and the law. Now that had changed with the Divorce Law Reform Act (1969). Fiona, with little income at first, had been able to return to teaching and create a secure and loving home environment for her boys which felt more peaceful than the one in which they lived in the years leading to their parents' separation. Over the years the church had been a tremendous support providing listening ears and practical assistance. The boys had been helped particularly by their youth leaders who were like big brothers and sisters to them. Belonging to part of the Christian community enabled them to share in the life of a range of households including childless couples, two and one-parent families as well as single-person households. Graham and Jenny were glad of that.

Of course the grandchildren had not come through the upheaval in their family life unscathed. Initially there had been relative poverty with which to contend. Mum was busy handling her own emotions so that the daily routines of the home gave way to what felt like a chaotic lifestyle. Their school work seemed to suffer and they felt responsible for what had happened as so many children in their situation do. As far as the boys were concerned their grandparents had been like steady rocks through all of this, and the love and care of their extended church family had sustained them as they grieved the absence of daily contact with their Dad and as they went through the usual traumas of teenage life. It took them about two years to regain their equilibrium. One sadness was that they rarely saw their Dad now that he had remarried. Fiona had not remarried, unlike many divorced people who remarry and often bring children together in reconstituted families.

Jenny placed the flowers on the sideboard. No sooner had she done so than the doorbell rang again. Graham chuckled. 'Probably more flowers,' he said. And it was. These were from Ken and Yvonne. Ken was their eldest child. He and Yvonne had celebrated their silver wedding last year. It had been a happy occasion but Jenny thought Yvonne looked rather strained. The reason why became evident soon afterwards when Yvonne told her she was to lose her job. For many years this had been a dual income family. This had enabled them to both pay the mortgage and develop the business which Ken had bought. Yvonne had been unable to find another job, money was in short supply, and Jenny thought that the business may be under threat because of economic recession. However they would soon have the joyous experience of becoming grandparents.

Jenny sighed and said a prayer for Ken and the rest of his family. 'Mid-life can be a difficult time in a marriage,' she thought. 'I know from experience.'

If he had known his mother's thoughts Ken would have agreed. He was surprised when he recognised his jealousy when with Harry. Harry had everything ahead of him while he felt time was short and he was not going to achieve all that he wanted to do in life. The recession was hitting the business too. What sort of world was his grandchild being born into? He was not sure he wanted to be a grandad. It made him feel old. And then there was Yvonne's Mum. She was over eighty . . .

Yvonne was glad that she and Ken were able to talk to each other. Everything seemed to come at once. Losing her job had been a real blow not only financially but in terms of role, status and use of skills. She felt useless and lonely because friends and neighbours were not available in the daytime. In addition there was her mother to think about. She had always been an active, elderly person and very independent but the time had come when she needed more support. She and Ken were exploring the possibility of moving her mother to live nearby, or even with them, but with the business under threat was that wise?

Then there was Elizabeth. She would need support once the baby came. Yvonne felt pulled in two directions wanting to support both her mother and her daughter.

This was a difficult time of transition for Yvonne and Ken with a range of external factors affecting their marriage as well as their own physical and emotional states. The doctor had prescribed hormone replacement therapy for Yvonne and a holiday for Ken. They planned to have a day out together on their way to Jenny and Graham's Golden Wedding celebrations where they would be able to forget their own troubles as they rejoiced with others they loved.

'We'd better be getting into our best bibs and tuckers,' said Graham. 'We want to be ready when Elaine arrives.' 'Hadn't realised the time,' replied Jenny. 'Must look my best today.'

Elaine would arrive soon. She was coming to stay for the weekend and had arranged to take them to their celebratory dinner.

Graham straightened his tie and decided he was ready. He sat down to wait for Jenny and the familiar sound of Elaine's car as it pulled into the driveway. He thought of their youngest daughter. Elaine lived a fulfilling life. She had not married but she had a warm, comfortable home to which her friends seemed to gravitate and a job which she felt was a vocation. Her nephews and niece loved her. She had always been a significant person in their lives.

Elaine had chosen to be single rather than marry someone who did not share her faith. It had been a hard decision but the best one for her. She was convinced of that but she understood the pressure some Christian singles feel because the opportunity of marriage has not come their way, or they have been widowed or divorced, or because they are scared of sexual intimacy or are attracted to those of the same sex. Glib teaching does not help but concerned and sensitive pastoral support does.

The car horn sounded. Elaine had arrived. There were hugs all round and then Graham and Jenny were off to join the rest of the family. Family life has its ups and downs. Today was an 'up day'. At the meal table Graham whispered to Jenny, 'Haven't we got a wonderful family? God's been good to us.' Jenny sighed with pleasure as she observed her extended three and soon-to-be-four generation family.

Theirs is a dispersed extended family living in different types of family units and in various geographical locations. Frequent and regular contact is made between the households. This is the most common type of family to be found in Britain today accounting for about half the population. A few people live in extended families which are located close to each other giving mutual assistance (one in eight adults) while the rest belong to dispersed families which do not keep regular contact.

Martin Fletcher slipped into his study to finalise his sermon for the following day. This was his usual pattern on a Saturday. First the weddings and then the finalising of the sermon before the football match started. He liked to share that interest with his own sons at the weekend.

Tomorrow the church was joining Jenny and Graham in celebrating their golden wedding with cake and coffee after the service. Martin wanted it to be a special occasion for them as well as for the rest of the congregation. He was aware that there were those whose experience of family was painful but who longed for acceptance, a sense of belonging and love which is the 'stuff' of positive family life. He and his leadership team were currently preparing sermon and housegroup materials on the subject of family life, which they hoped would help the congregation to learn more about the purpose and mission of family in the kingdom of God.

Over the ten years he had been at the church Jenny and Graham's family had become a sign of hope to Martin. Like all families it was fallen, as well as touched and affected by the culture and trends of the day, but its members knew and experienced the grace of God. They recognised God as the God of process, the One who is with them in all circumstances and who is able to sustain and to help in times of difficulty and need. Yes, they made mistakes and had to live with the consequences of them but at heart most individuals in the family loved God, knew his forgiveness, and together wanted to serve him. This had become evident during the painful period of Fiona's separation and divorce. They wrestled with Scripture. They supported each other, loved, belonged, prayed, forgave and accepted. In different ways they supported Fiona and the boys. They also looked to the wider family of the local church for further help. Fiona's one-parent family became a healthy unit within their wider kinship family which was itself within the family of faith.

Christians in families are related not only through marriage and kinship but through the blood of Jesus. They are brothers and sisters in Christ, adopted into God's family. When Christians in families grasp this fact they may relate differently. Things might be different if they related as older brothers or sisters of their children and grandchildren recognising that they have joined them on the journey of faith towards God and on with him. Then they would concentrate on family relationships rather than structure and role. Martin thought that would be a good thing.

While some Christians argued strongly for the protection of the family, often the nuclear family only, Jesus challenged families of all types to put first the kingdom of God and made apparently outlandish statements about his own kinship group. 'Who is my mother? Who are my brothers?' Then he pointed to his disciples and said, 'Look! Here are my mother and my brothers! Whoever does what my Father in heaven wants him to do is my brother, my sister, and my mother' (Matt 12: 48–50).

It seemed to Martin that Jesus was calling the family into the service of the kingdom of God. Family has a purpose but Jesus does not give it a tight definition. He calls people to quality relating, to faithfulness and commitment; to relationship with God and each other and by God's grace to the creation of a covenant community in which people give and receive love, affection, care, forgiveness, nurture and healing. And these gifts are not just for the members of the family but for all whom that family touches – the next-door neighbour, colleagues, those at the school gate – for just as God, the Father, Son and Spirit, has opened up his family so that all families on earth may be adopted into it, Christians in families are to nurture open family life so that they may be lights or examples that bring hope to others. Authentic family life for Christians with all its faults will show the grace of God at work. Christians are called to a family life which exists in the world and is a sign of God's covenant and grace thus bringing hope and inspiration to other families.

Martin thought of Jenny and Graham's family again. They had not read all the books or studied the theology but they were doing the theology of family all the time by being Christian and working out their family life with God and each other.

They were concerned about pressures on families caused by unemployment, poor housing, isolation and poverty. They had a heart for those sinned against and the victims of circumstances. Just last week Graham had gently challenged Martin to encourage Christians in families to be more informed and involved in local affairs as they affect the family. Graham might be celebrating his golden wedding but he had not retired.

Looking at his watch Martin realised that he must sharpen up his thoughts for the sermon. He jotted down his major points:

1. God created family when he created human beings like himself to live in relationship with himself and with each other in kinship groups.
2. The rebellion of human beings described in Genesis 3 resulted in the relationship with God being broken and the disruption of kinship groupings.
3. The image of God may still be seen in fallen individuals and families because God created them and continues to be gracious to them.
4. Jesus has made relationship with God the Father possible for individuals and their kinship groups as originally intended. He can bring them into a faith relatedness that transcends kinship relatedness and lives on in the coming kingdom of God and leads to wholeness.
5. Christ brings redemption using the material to hand, which means working with the fallen families we have rather than the perfect ones we would like to have.
6. Family life is intended to be the most intimate experience of the kingdom of God on earth, one in which God is worshipped and in which the members love, relate and reach out to others.
7. All families need support, nurture and a wider community to belong to. The local church is uniquely placed to be this community.

Earthed with a few illustrations Martin thought there would be more than enough for one sermon there. He was conscious, however, that there was much work to be done working out the practical implications of this in homes and churches affected by today's trends in family life. 'That's enough for now,' he thought, 'but it has left me with a lot to think about.' So he wrote:

'For future consideration'

A FOUR-GENERATION DISPERSED KINSHIP FAMILY
(Graham & Jenny's family)

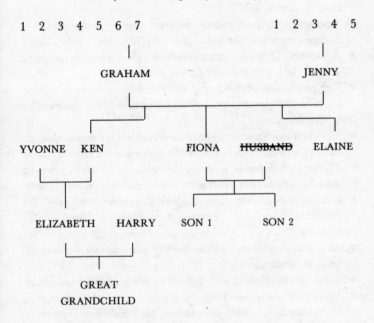

FIVE HOUSEHOLDS:

1 Married couple – Graham and Jenny
2 Married couple – Yvonne and Ken
3 Nuclear family – Elizabeth, Harry and child
4 One-parent family – Fiona and sons
5 Single person household – Elaine

- The trend is towards this type of family. Ninety-five per cent of adults belong to such extended families, the majority of which are geographically dispersed but have regular contact, e.g. weekly.
- More four generation families.
- Greater longevity of life with marriages expected to last longer.
- Families are getting smaller.
- Greater geographical spread of families.
- Rapid increase in the numbers of elderly.
- Growth in one-person household (twenty-five per cent of all households in 1987).
- Teenage marriages have declined significantly probably because more people cohabit before marriage.
- About half of never-married women cohabit before marriage while others cohabit but do not marry.
- The proportion of children (twenty-five per cent) born outside marriage is increasing though most of these are registered by both parents.
- Divorce rates are increasing. Marriages last for shorter periods of time and one in five children experience parental divorce.
- There is a substantial increase in lone-parent families bringing poverty while other families become relatively more affluent.
- Grandparents are the major providers of care for grandchildren who increasingly belong to dual-worker families.
- Increasing numbers of children live in households where the head is unemployed.
- Most caring of the elderly is done by female family members.
- Young people live at home longer with more of them staying in full-time education or enrolled on training schemes.
- Homelessness is increasing.
- Divorced people cohabit for longer periods between marriages.
- Substantial numbers of divorced people remarry within five years. Remarriages are at greater risk of dissolution than first marriages especially if the couple have children from previous marriages.
- Most marriages last ''til death do us part' and the vast

majority (eighty-eight per cent) value their family very highly. They do not, however, think that shared religious or political beliefs are important when choosing a marriage partner.

Questions

In what ways is my family life an experience of the kingdom of God? What might need changing to make it more so?

In what ways are we and others developing relationships in the church and wider community that will enrich and nurture our own family lives as well as those of others?

Which of the trends above might Christians see as welcome and which unwelcome? Which trends, if any, may they want to accommodate to?

If families are increasingly small and geographically spread how can they continue to provide care for children or the aged and housebound? What role might the church have here?

What more might the church do to support families through times of change and transitions that they all go through, e.g. marriage, birth of child, leaving home, loss or bereavement?

In what ways might the local church improve its family life education?

There was a knock at the door. 'Time for the match, Dad. Are you coming?'

Sources

Kathleen Kiernan and Malcolm Wicks, *Family change and future policy* (Family Policy Studies Centre).

Mark Abrams, David Gerard and Noel Timms (eds), *Values and Social Change in Britain* (Macmillan Press, 1985).

Findings of European Value Systems Study Group: family life section, 1992.

5

Youth Culture

Arkle Bell

> Children nowadays are real tyrants, they no longer
> stand up when their elders come into the room.
>
> Socrates

In recent history many have argued that 'youth', 'adolescence'
and 'teenager' are post-war concepts. We have talked in graphic
terms of 'youth culture' and have seen young people as either
'heroes' or 'horrors'. During these last fifty years we have seen
the churches becoming less and less successful in winning the
hearts and minds of young people, so much so that the term
'young people' in many of our churches refers to anyone younger
than ourselves and on Sunday mornings as anyone we cannot
accommodate in the learning process of a graduate delivered
sermon.

The term 'YOUTH' is, then, a movable feast in most of our
academic and social definitions. We are faced with psychological
definitions which relate to puberty and maturation and the period
defined as adolescence. In sociology it may relate to status in
a given society. For many of us these are a collection of words

used to define a group of people with whom adult society has tenuous links and the Christian Church is no exception to this.

During twenty years of active work with young people, I have seen our concerns for the young adult diminish. As a fourteen year old (in the 60s) I was involved in a number of groups, both church based and para church, in which at the local level, 14s – 21s were actively involved in evangelism and provided with good youth work bases that reached Christians and their friends in the community. My concern in the 90s is that many churches have become so involved with the families in the church, those primarily who are thirty to forty in age range, that the comfortable environment created for them is alien to young people approaching maturity. The report 'Christian England' shows many thousands of young people leaving our churches each year but what is the environment they are moving into? Where do the majority of young people find friendship, support and leisure pursuits?

I shall attempt to answer with the use of a number of case studies.

John

John is eighteen; he lives in a northern industrial town. He left school at sixteen – he is just coming to the end of a course at a local college of further education. Home is with Mum on a local council estate and Dad left five years ago to find a job in London. In the early days Dad commuted weekly but now he never comes home and neither does the money. John has no hope of finding a job, or at least that is how he feels, as most of his friends are jobless. As he has no job John is able to spend a major part of his free time at the local sports centre where he is a member of the local snooker team and football club. He often spends the rest of the evening at the leisure centre bar. Weekends are spent in town at one of three discos or clubs offering the latest in pop music, the stronger the rock beat the better.

John's loyalties are very much to his own close group of male friends involved in the football club and their latest girl friends.

John's view of the future would be to find a job locally and probably marry. If he could, he would prefer to get a council house, but really he is not thinking that far ahead.

Tim

Tim is coming up to twenty and is in his final degree year in Business Studies at a polytechnic, about two hours by train from his South East home. Mum remarried about five years ago and, as well as his seventeen year old sister, they now have a three year old half-brother. Mum's new husband is a rep and dotes on the little boy. Tim and his sister, Jill, get on with their own lives. She is studying 'A' levels at the local sixth form college. During the week Tim spends a lot of his time in his mate's rooms in 'halls', chatting and listening to music. Weekends he may go to a party or the student bar. He is concerned about his sister as she and her friends seem to be getting heavily involved in the rave and ecstasy scene. The relationship between mother and daughter really seems to have broken down and neither sees any clear direction ahead, either in their own relationship or for Jill's future. The pressure in her sixth form is more about partying than scholarship.

However, Tim is starting to think more clearly and a number of options are open to him, particularly as he is a good athlete. A number of American universities are interested in him and he could pursue his academic studies.

On the other hand, he is aware of the problems in the 'two thirds world' and has been talking seriously with VSO and a number of aid agencies.

Jill

Jill comes from an affluent middle-class background, living in the Midlands with her parents, both of whom are well established in their careers. Father is a doctor and mother teaches in a local school.

Jill is about to take her GCSEs. She is an active member of her local county wildlife trust, she is a vegetarian and has loose links with the local church through its youth club, which has a wide ranging social programme. She has links with one of the animal liberation groups, of which her boyfriend, from the local college, is a member. Occasionally she has been involved with hunt saboteurs.

Her two younger brothers are still at primary school. They tend to interfere with her social life as her parents think she is a convenient baby-sitter when they go to the golf club.

Jill's taste in music is wide. She plays cello in the school orchestra. She has loose links also with some so called 'New Age' influences.

Paul

Paul's parents moved here in the sixties from the West Indies and Africa. Paul clearly sees himself as black British. His parents have long since rejected the white English churches. Dad has no time for organised religion and Mum attends a black majority Pentecostal denomination.

For years Paul has been torn between his parents' belief and non-belief. His mother's youngest brother was unable to cope with Britain and eventually gained an engineering degree in East Germany before moving to Angola in the early 80s, to be involved in the 'struggle'.

Paul sees his uncle as a hero and wants to follow in his footsteps. The 90s, however, do not appear to give a young unemployed black teenager the openings. Recently he has joined a small group of black Muslims in the area, hoping that this will answer his spiritual and social needs.

Jade

At work Jade has formed a relationship with a young Asian man of similar age. However, his background is considerably different from hers. Not only is his family from a poorer background so that an adequate dowry would be out of the question, but they are also of different religious persuasions. This does not matter

71

to them as they are both fairly secular and westernised in their own way, enjoying the company of their white colleagues in their works social club. Dancing and pop music are part of their way of life.

However both of them realise that eventually family pressure will come to bear as they attempt to be more open about their relationship. They feel trapped, unable to go to their parents and reticent about being fully integrated into white society, with all its flaws. Their ultimate fear is that Jade will be sent back to her uncle in the Asian sub-continent.

Gail

Gail ran away from home when she was fourteen. Now eighteen, she has a baby girl and lives in a council flat in one of the poorer London boroughs.

In order to make ends meet she regularly uses the local church's playgroup and lunch club. Her boyfriend, the baby's father, occasionally drops in when he's short of money.

Gail is involved in prostitution on a part-time basis in order to pay for the little extras she needs for the baby. Twice a week she has a babysitter who comes in while she goes down to King's Cross. Gail's flat is poorly furnished and the cupboards are only well stocked when the Giro arrives, fortnightly.

On occasions Gail thinks back to home and her older sister who is married, trying to pluck up courage to make contact again.

Jim

Jim is sixteen and lives with his parents on a farm. The nearest village is five miles away and the nearest town twenty miles. The cinema has just closed. Occasionally one of the local pubs will put on a disco. The farm will not support Jim when he leaves school in the summer, so he is hoping to go to college in the town – his only means of transport being a 50cc moped. Although the town is small, around 30,000 people, there have been a number of disturbances between young people and the police in recent years. Jim spends most of his evenings with a group of young men around the local village pub.

None of these young people are typical, but are cameos of situations I have come across in the last ten years.

Education and training have been key planks of Government policy but the various employment and educational initiatives have merely added to the complexity of life and to the pressures on young people. On top of this, the scientifically and technologically adept workforce has still not emerged into the workplace. In many areas less than 10% of young people now leave school at sixteen. But as yet there appears to be no bright light at the end of the tunnel. Just as there are good stories provided in the press about employment prospects, many young people feel cheated and abused by poorly funded training programmes in employer led schemes. To make matters worse, in many of our large cities youth homelessness is rising.

But where does this place the church and its environment with young people?

During 1990/91 I conducted two pieces of research amongst young people, churches and youth workers. A brief resumé of this was published in 'The Times' in April 1992. The reader needs to reflect on the preceding case study material in the light of the evidence from this research which is reported in the remainder of the chapter.

Alongside the research project, the Department for Education was also conducting a series of ministerial conferences with the aim of promoting an agreed curriculum for youth work in England and Wales. Coopers Lybrand were used as consultants and three conferences took place in the years around the 1992 General Election.

The churches

Although the major part of the research into the churches' involvement with young people took place within a particular Association of the Baptist Union, the results correlated with previous work done by Leslie Francis in Lancashire[1] and with the 1992 Marc Europe report 'Christian England'[2].

So who are these Christians, which young people do they work with and how? Thirty-one churches of the sixty-five in the Association took part in the review. Almost all of the larger churches, who tend to be fairly self-sufficient, were not involved in the research. In trying to identify who Baptists are, we looked at their theological background and their social class, in terms of both membership and leadership. The recent publication *'Christian' England* shows that Baptists view themselves as very little different from other Christians. In theological background nearly 50% see themselves as evangelical, 12% identify some strong charismatic influence and 38% have a broad Christian allegiance. Both in terms of leadership and membership, responses indicate a preponderance of the white-collar, professional and retired groups. Blue collar workers scored well under 20% in both membership and leadership.

These figures are not surprising, for Leslie Francis showed in Lancashire that there was an imbalance in social class, when it came to church involvement, in favour of the professional and white-collar groups.[3] Following this trend it is not surprising that Baptists have high educational aspirations for their young people and probably attract young people with a similar academic and social background to their own.

The fact that 48.4% of the churches would expect their young people to go to college is, in our society, a surprising result, when National Government only expect, in their long term forecasts, to reach a target of 20%. It may of course be that the question was not fully understood and includes some who may be attending colleges of Further Education. However, looking at the social background of the members of churches, there would not seem to be a significant deviation in this direction.

Who are they working with?

Predominantly, the churches were working with young people in the 13/17 year age range, often in very small groups. Only six churches had groups with more than ten young people of the same sex in a group. The only large-scale youth work reported was in a church where they employ a member as a part-time paid youth worker.

Disabled young people and those from ethnic minorities play no significant part in the lives of the churches studied. The only large minority ethnic youth group was in a church which had a substantial number of young gypsies involved in the church. We are aware of another church working co-operatively with other denominations in inner city multi-ethnic youth work. White Christians need to be aware of the significant work being done by black majority churches and often with older young people.

Whilst contact with 13/17 year olds may seem encouraging, we need to take note of the fact that more than half of the churches had no formal contact with 18/23 year olds.

Of the other churches the majority had contact with very small numbers, in general less than five in any group.

This downward trend is not exclusively Baptist for *'Christian' England* notes a decline of 150,000 during the ten year period 1979–1989, in the main denominational groups. Only the Independent Churches showed any increase, but much of this must be construed as transferred membership, as the overall drop was so large.

How are they working?

There is no question in recent years, that two of the major parts of Christian youth work have either taken a back seat in the churches, or have become vehicles of children's work rather than youth work, when youth work is defined as work with teenagers and young adults.

These two would be:
 (i) The uniformed organisations
(ii) the traditional youth club, or any of its derivatives encouraged by the youth service.

The youth work of the Baptist churches researched was church based, youth fellowship style work. From the evidence we must presume that this was primarily for those who already consider themselves to be Christians. Very few of the young people are encouraged to take leadership roles. Only in the case of Sunday

School have more than 10% of the churches offered young people leadership experience.

One leading Baptist commented, whilst being interviewed for this research, 'their geographical location in numbers are in the suburbs and so they are mostly content to work with their own children and keep them as long as they can, until they lose them. After that they hold up their hands in horror and say, "Help!" '

There was no clear evidence of Baptist churches serving their communities' youth. It would appear to be that they are content to work with their own young people before they leave for college and make their own decisions about Christian faith and denominational affiliation. Given the evidence from *'Christian' England*, this gives cause for concern for Baptists do not seem to have the means to hold onto their own young people, let alone develop styles of youth work which attract others.

As well as local church provision, we investigated the use of events organised by local and national Christian bodies. Popularity for events was high, with over 68% of the churches supporting local Christian music events.

This was followed closely by three other styles of events, one local and two national. These are events organised by the local Baptist Youth Committee (48%), Greenbelt Christian Arts Festival (38.9%) and Spring Harvest (35.5%). These events tend to have an evangelical bias.

A major disappointment denominationally, must be the lack of support for specifically Baptist, national youth events and opportunities to serve others.

Home Mission Task Force and Christmas Cracker, a series of cafés raising funds for world relief, were supported by less than 20% of the churches. Both the Baptist Missionary Society and the Baptist Youth Ministry Department need to take note of the fact that nobody replying to the survey in the local churches attended the National Residential Event at Windermere and only 16% of the churches attended the multi media 28/19 Tour.

The evidence seems to show conclusively that the Baptist young people have a greater tendency to attend events when accompanied by youth workers. This is particularly true when the event is local or regional. The exceptions are Spring Harvest, where because of the style of the event family attendance is probably more important, and Greenbelt, where the peer group is a significant motivating factor. We have no statistical evidence to back these assertions; they are based on the researcher's active involvement in both events.

Consultation

In recent years churches have had to make decisions as to whether their young people are the 'Church of Today' or the 'Church of Tomorrow'. In youth work terms, many agencies are attempting to find ways of improving and developing the active participation of young people. The Baptist Union has, over recent years, attempted to develop the Association of Baptist Youth. In this survey none of the churches made specific reference to the Association's existence and work.

When asked whether they had consulted their young people 55% of the churches responded positively. The methods and frequency with which they did this varied considerably; ministers, deacons and youth workers were involved in varying degrees. Half of the churches responding positively, used their youth workers as the most frequent means of consultation.

One leading Baptist said, 'My feeling is that people do not understand the sub-culture that young people, not simply those outside the church but young people inside the church, are actually into'.

Young people in the community

Having seen the state of a particular denomination in its relationship with young people, it is important to obtain a wider Christian perspective. Commenting recently on one of the churches in the Liverpool Diocese, Bishop David Sheppard noted that the local church members had no real links with the local youth centre. The curate was the only member of the congregation ever to have been in the building.

As unemployment remains high, as materialism becomes the perceived dominant religion, as designer drugs become more widely available we need to have a broader understanding of young people. When civil unrest is always identified with young people, we need to ask significant questions in our communities.

Two examples from Bristol's Hartcliffe Estate, which saw its shopping centre in flames in the summer of 1992, are revealing. The first involves a *Panorama* programme about young people and alcohol abuse.

The programme planning had started with the full co-operation of local youth workers. However, the young people on whom the programme focussed were extremely vulnerable young people, from unstable backgrounds. The impression given was that they had been regularly consuming large quantities of cider. The youth workers knew this was untrue and attempted to mediate. Nevertheless, the programme went ahead showing, what was really their bravado as if it were their normal way of life.

The second example relates to the way television reported the 1992 disturbances on the estate.

I watched the local television news on the following morning. Within one hour the report on the same piece of film had changed from men leaving the pubs to young people or youths. With such standards of reporting how can we be sure what is the truth? This causes old people to be in fear of violence from young people, yet over 75% of violent crime is by young adults on young adults. So what is a true picture of young people? What follows is an attempt to develop a better understanding as we look at their relationships with youth workers.

In this piece of research the youth workers were all practising Christians and the young people were members of youth centres from a variety of backgrounds across the south-west of England. The young people interviewed were fifteen and over. In terms of social class, almost 70% came from a blue collar background and over 75% lived in owner occupied accommodation – possibly a result of the Thatcher Government's encouragement to buy council houses.

Obviously as Christian researchers, we were interested in the beliefs as well as the practices of the young people we studied. Over a third of them professed to be Anglicans, whilst a similar number had no church allegiance. The findings are presented here in four areas.

1 Popular music and its influences

Popular music is widely assumed to be a significant element of youth culture but there is actually much debate about the place of music in the lives of young people. Steve Goddard, former editor of 'Buzz' magazine, has reminded us how some church leaders have expressed deep concern about the impact which rock music has on young people. The sociologists, Prinsley and Rosenbaum, have also recognised that, 'regardless of the evidence, that most youths do not comprehend most of the lyrics and the tunes they listen to, popular music may have important symbolic meaning for them'.

What is the evidence from the young people we researched? It supports a variety of conclusions, some predictable and others controversial. Contemporary pop music is as highly rated as we would expect. Classical music did not feature highly in the interest of many. There was some evidence of 'a working class preference for Top Twenty' observed by Willis.

The principal area of controversy relates to the impact the lyrics and the life-styles of pop stars have on young people. On the one hand, the adults we questioned think that young people are influenced. They are supported in this view by some social scientists who suggest a link between the sexual references in some pop lyrics and changing moral standards and behaviour. But the young people and the youth workers in our study strongly disagreed with this view.

Experienced observers of the youth scene will be aware of the wide variety of musical styles that are lumped together as 'pop'. This suggests that we should be cautious about blanket generalisations. We also need to remember that popular music is the product of an industry which is not under the control of young people. Michael Brake, whose insights into youth culture are so helpful, has observed that, 'all pop styles and stars are products of the industry rather than authentic statements of young people's feeling and interests'. We also need to remember that one fashion designer admitted recently to having invented the whole 'punk' era because it seemed valid in economic terms! This makes a nonsense of the image of 'punk' as the cultural expression of disaffected young people.

2 Sexual relationships and attitudes

This whole area is changing rapidly. We did not ask about anyone's own sexual practice, but rather their attitude towards various aspects of sexual ethics. We will show clearly that Mayerson's statement that 'permissive society' always seems to be 'other people and adolescence'.

In many cultures, virginity prior to marriage will be part of the religious culture for both men and women. Has this changed over recent years? How do the attitudes of young people differ from those of adult Christians?

In our sample only 8% of the young people thought virginity before marriage is important. Their attitudes were considerably more permissive on this issue than the adult sample.

On the gay issue, however, differences in attitude between the generations were less stark. 64% of the young people were prepared to accept gay people in their friendship group whereas amongst adults the figure was only 45.5%. Some of the young men interviewed were highly intolerant and used such comments as, 'they're queer', 'disgusting, ought to be shot', 'ought to be chopped off. That's what gave us AIDS'. When faced with a case study which might relate to them, young working class males showed a high level of intolerance. Faced with the same case study, young women responded with a more tolerant view.

It was noticeable throughout this section of the research, that youth workers typically took a middle position. One youth worker said, when commenting on the gay case study used in the research, 'They are going to come into the youth centre anyway – there is no way you can ban them from the centre if they are gay or lesbian. But I know it is going to cause uproar with the kids in the centre'.

3 Drugs and society

Whether it is beer for the worker on the assembly line, a 'highball' for the high powered executive, or a sleeping tablet for his housebound wife, the aim is the same – 'to forget!' So says Upson in Chapter 10 of 'Adolescents'.

We saw all this and more in our results. Many young people

would also see drugs and particularly alcohol as being part of their togetherness. Only one person admitted to the use of cannabis. None of the young people admitted to the use of hard drugs, even though a number of them lived in areas where hard drugs were supposed to be readily available.

Socially accepted drugs are widely used by all. These were tea and coffee, alcohol – beers, wines and spirits, and tobacco. The young people over a period of a year had seen a change in usage – a downward trend. The most significant change was in the use of tobacco even though it was still a regularly used drug.

In the interview situations, the case study brought out an acceptance of the use of socially acceptable drugs. The young people in particular had a view of drugs which progressed from the use of the acceptable, tea and coffee, through alcohol and cannabis to hard drugs. However, the youth workers were the widest drug users, with over 35% having used cannabis, as well as other reports of solvents and magic mushrooms being used. As in most cases there was no longer any use, the youth workers obviously felt free to share their experiences. It may be that the young people were unwilling to share their actual experiences at this time.

It could be said from the experience of the youth workers that careful education has played a part in their behavioural change. However, we need to be aware of the dominant values in our present society.

There is, it appears, a general ambivalence across society in the use of the more acceptable drugs. Young people are caught in this. Their apparent anti-social behaviour on occasions should not give rise to a law and order response. If the lives of the youth workers give us any guidance, education and relationship building seem to be important.

4 Christian belief and wider values

It was very openly our intention to work with the concepts of Christian belief. We were trying to ascertain how far young people understand and accept orthodox Christianity.

The picture the young people gave us was of a confused view

of spiritual life in which Christianity was supposed to be part of the social and ethical undergirding. Their experience was one of being wholly Christian.

We saw earlier that 56% of young people would call themselves Anglican or Christian and 56% of them profess a belief in God, but only 20% indicate that they attend church regularly and only 12% said they had been to church that week. This all contrasts strongly with the Christian youth workers.

The young people seem to have mixed views about Jesus: 72% indicate they believe that Jesus was a good man; 80% believe He is the Son of God; only 28% believe He is God; 68% believe He rose from the dead, but only 36% think He is alive today – a popular Christian affirmation.

Belief in miracles, prayer and the supernatural had high scores. The young people also had an ambivalent view of other faiths, seeing some form of godliness in all expressions of religion.

There clearly is a spiritual dimension to the lives of young people, but it does not seem to be harnessed by any organisation, least of all the church. Spiritual development is on the agenda of Youth Service, but there seems to be no clear attempt to analyse the need. Young people dabble in other faiths and make spiritual explorations in uncharted waters.

Orthodox Christianity in the House of Lords amended the force of the Education Reform Act. The pressures of the former Bishop of London, Graham Leonard, or Baroness Cox would not be those that youth work agencies would endorse. Enforced religious observance and education does not fit within the ethos of youth service, where informal methods are to the fore in educational methodology.

The research questionnaire also contained some value questions. The young people showed a high degree of altruism on such issues as:

(a) Atomic or Chemical Weapons
(b) Famine
(c) Greed
(d) The Environment.

Here their views were very similar to the adults. All showed a positive response to the dangers in these areas. Maybe these issues could be the starting point for belief and values development.

All the groups saw that being a member of a church should help us explore our morals and beliefs. But neither the youth workers nor the young people saw the church as being the most important agent in setting our moral standards. In interviews the young people identified family and friends as being the major groups in this area.

At this point it is worth quoting John Ellis of the Shalom Youth Centre, Grimsby, where John is both parish priest and youth worker. As youth worker, he believes that we, 'must be able to demonstrate that informal education is an appropriate vehicle for communicating the Christian message'. Recently John and the church have seen young people taking an active interest in less formal worship, as they explore issues of spirituality and faith.

The way ahead

In conclusion, we believe that it is fairly clear that there is no dominant youth culture. Over the past ten years we have seen the rise and fall of 'punk' then the 'goths' and in the early 90s the growth of 'rave' which has also brought in its own worship style seen in various forms at Greenbelt '92. We may raise various questions about the use of particular music forms, but the church has a history of redeeming the music of the day and creating vibrant Christian worship. Music is just one dimension in the vast tapestry of youth cultures.

As Christians concerned for our world, we need to have a godly concern for our young people, whether in the Christian community or outside of it.

It is encouraging to see a growing number of Christians concerned with homelessness, but is this just a short term interest as we saw in the 70s and 80s with unemployment?

Some years ago at a Frontier Youth Trust conference in the Irish Republic a Jesuit priest urged a group of youth workers to be more like Jesus. By this he meant we should spend time learning about our community, and the young people in it, before launching into a mission project. He told of his own experience in Dublin, where he and other brothers lived on a difficult housing estate, before doing any work there. Now a number of years later, they are involved actively with young people in the drug scene, as well as being the catalyst for a number of responses to homelessness among young people.

The churches have, in general, failed the young adult in our society. This situation needs redressing, or by the end of the century, the church will be catering for old age pensioners in lunch clubs and mums who need playgroups and toddlers clubs. Each congregation needs to actively research its neighbourhood, identifying groups of young people and their obvious needs.

Traditionally some areas of youth work have been defined as 'association', 'development' or 'challenge' and we may have even more Christian jargon slogans. We should not be discouraged by a different jargon, but be aiming to work co-operatively with others, both within the Christian community and without, to enable young people to reach their full potential.

Many times in the past, the church has been committed to youth work, only when it sees fairly immediate results. Our view of Christian faith seems to be built on the consumer values of our society and not on any well thought out biblical base. The results of this action may take us into areas where we feel uncomfortable. However, for the sake of the Gospel, our interaction, not just with Christian young people but also with a wide range of adults with different skills and interests, needs to be in our communities offering friendship, direction and resources. Doing this may well mean taking on the role of substitute brothers and sisters, parents, aunts and uncles or grandparents. The good youth worker is not characterised by age proximity, but by commitment to young people and their predicaments.

We need to know our neighbourhood and its young people. We need to know the resources and agencies available to them and us; know our own skills and limitations; to train according to need, and then move out by the power of the Spirit, to service a forgotten world!

Notes

1   L. J. Francis, *Teenagers and the Church* (Collins Liturgical Publications, London, 1984).
2   P. Brierley, *Christian England* (MARC Europe, London, 1991).
3   L. J. Francis, *Teenagers and the Church*.

Further reading

M. Brake, *The Sociology of Youth Culture and Youth Subcultures* (Routledge and Kegan Paul, London, 1980).
P. Brierley, *Christian England* (MARC Europe, London, 1991).
D. Day and P. May, *Teenage Beliefs* (Lion Publishing, Oxford, 1991).
L. J. Francis, *Teenagers and the Church* (Collins Liturgical Publications, London, 1984).
M. Wroe (ed), *Dancing in the Dragon's Jaws* (Greenbelt Festivals Ltd., London, 1988).

6

Education

George Oliver

The general election of April 1992, leaving the Conservative Party with a reduced but still adequate overall majority of twenty-one, makes it likely that for the five years to 1997 we may expect, broadly speaking, a continuation of the same education policies and trends as we have experienced throughout the eighties. No radical change of direction is likely. The Conservative governments of the past thirteen years have taken a great deal of interest in education; there was a piece of education legislation in almost every year of the eighties. Much of their work deals with the realms of Higher and/or Further Education, vitally important in many ways to the life of the nation. But in this short essay the main emphasis will be on the education which happens, or ought to happen, in schools, and which therefore affects the children of almost the entire population.

What happens in schools, however, needs to be seen in context. Maybe it is obvious that education is a lifelong process; it happens wherever people are learning. And much of the most important learning takes place in our earliest years, before any schooling begins. Reflect for a moment on what we expect a normal child to have mastered in the first years of its life. To stand unaided, to walk and run, to co-ordinate hand movements, to acquire a sense of rhythm; all of these are massive steps forward in learning. Some of them we mark with delight in our family life. Baby's first steps are a matter for celebration. Even more impressive is the way the small child, in its first years, develops its command of speech. From the inarticulate newborn baby to the five year old who can make his/her wants known most effectively in words, and beyond that can discuss volcanoes, or wild animals, recite from memory the whole text of a favourite story and ask shrewd questions about God, is an enormous stride in educational terms. And as a 'spin-off' from this skill we expect the five year old to have the right words to enable it to name colours accurately, and to begin to talk about numbers.

Starting from scratch, a child makes more striking advances in learning in its first five years than probably at any other period in its life. And this learning usually takes place within the patterns of ordinary home and social life. It is so common that we tend to take it for granted. But no learning happens automatically. A 'complete' loving family environment has the potential to *provide*, however unselfconsciously, the circumstances and situations necessary for a child's healthy educational development – children are talked to, listened to, read to. They are encouraged and praised for every new step forward. Their attempts at communication are rewarded by understanding and corrected with love and approval. A home can be, and often is in these early years, something approaching an ideal educational environment. It can also be very far distant from the ideal. If children are not talked to, played with, listened to, encouraged, their development may be slowed or even almost completely halted. The conditions which came to light in the Romanian orphanages rightly shocked us. Many of those children revealed on our television screens will never develop normally because the necessary early steps of their education, all the accompaniments of a normal childhood, have never happened.

But a phenomenon of our own society, attested by many infant teachers, is the number of children entering school whose physical and social skills and language development are way below what they ought to be. The causes of this situation are many. Inner

city life in the eighties and nineties does not easily provide
scope for social meeting and safe play for toddlers. Single parent
households, or those where both parents work full time, may
limit their children's 'quality time' with Mum and Dad.
Nursery school provision within the national education system
is patchy. There is a demand and a need for more if children,
especially disadvantaged children, are to reach the starting line
equipped to take up the opportunities offered by school. Even
before we consider schooling, there is here a situation which
Christian people need to take seriously, the more so perhaps,
because it is outside the experience of so many of us. In the
circumstances of the modern 'market-place' there are losers.
The unemployed and low paid may find it difficult to provide
stimulating environments for their children. Can the rest of
us, in secular terms, *afford* not to *pay* for the provision of
facilities which will to some extent even up the inequalities.
And as Christians, are we not committed to care in a special
way for the needy among us (Matt. 25:31–46, Luke 16:19–31,
Jas 2:1–4).

Schooling in this country is universal (more or less[1] from five
to eleven years. Its importance can be overstated. In fact its
influence operates alongside three other major factors in the life
of most modern young people, home, peer groups and the mass
media. Maybe for many it is not the most important of the four.
But it certainly is important. We send our children to school
basically because in the complexity of modern life there are things
they need to learn which informal education at home among
friends cannot usually provide. We send them with the positive
hope and expectation that they will benefit from the process. For
eleven years, often more, teachers will guide their development,
influence their moral growth, direct much of their reading and
thinking and overall have a considerable effect on their
acquisition of beliefs and values.

As Christians, how then should we see education as a whole
and schooling in particular? A starting point may be Jesus'
proclamation 'I have come that they may have life, and have
it to the full' (John 10:10). This is an 'entitlement' statement.
What Jeus requires for us is something we have no right to deny
to anyone. But a full life implies scope to discover and develop

our gifts in ways which fit in with God's purposes. It implies, also, the opportunity, unhindered, to come to a saving knowledge of the Lord. Jesus' rebuke to the disciples who prevented children from approaching him takes on a further significance in the educational setting (Mark 10:13–16).

The education process, seen as a whole, must for us Christians centre on three things. It must aim at enabling people to experience 'fullness of life'; that is the discovery and development of the talents of mind and body given to us by God. Equally, it must seek to direct the use of those gifts in the way of righteousness, in obedience to God's commandments; this is the way of true freedom. Thirdly, it must for *everyone*, open up at least the possibility of entering into a saving relationship with God through Jesus Christ. We dare not regard any of these ingredients as an optional extra. But, we live in a society containing large numbers of people who believe differently from us; and the dominant philosophy of life in much of that society, and in many of its schools, is a form of unashamedly self-centred secularism concerned exclusively with the affairs of this world. In this situation, we must explore carefully the limits of what it is reasonable to ask from the national system of schooling. We cannot expect the ordinary county school to deliver a complete Christian educational 'package'. We must thoughtfully and prayerfully supplement, and sometimes challenge the impact of secular schools through our church based education programmes and in our Christian homes.

At the same time we must recognise that the great majority of young people will not be affected by church youth programmes and will not grow up in Christian homes. We cannot be content with a school education system, therefore, which rules out the eternal dimension or even simply ignores it. In our plural society we must at least work for an educational approach and content which fairly presents the Christian option as worthy of serious consideration.

A fully Christian view of education requires a much more detailed explanation both of what we want for the children of the Christian community and also what it is proper to ask for all children. The brief discussion above, however, will serve its purpose as an introduction to a consideration of current approaches to education, and what may be the Christian response to them.

Funding, fairness and faith

Underlying all the trends and fashions in schooling in the nineties is the steady pressure to turn our national network of primary and secondary schools into an essentially secular system. In his short biography of Lord Shaftesbury, J C Pollock records how in 1870, when many Christians were rejoicing at the triumph of obtaining for the first time a measure of state funding to help provide free elementary education for all, Shaftesbury was cast down by his perception that bringing in the state would in the end inevitably mean secularising schools[2]. The process took a long time. As late as 1944, Canon Spencer Leeson, in his Bampton lectures on 'Christian Education' in the aftermath of the 1944 Education Act could still seriously seek to claim the national education system as Christian[3]. But by the seventies and eighties such a claim would have been laughed out of court. Only in the church schools, Anglican and Roman Catholic, a smaller section of the total school provision than in 1944, though still considerable[4], do Christian values and beliefs inform the whole of school life by right. County schools which seek to be in some sense 'Christian' are a diminishing number. For the most part, in the county schools, questions about the place of Christianity in education are limited to the details of the religious education syllabus and the daily act of collective worship required by law[5]. Many Christians seem unaware of the extent of the shift towards secular assumptions in education which has taken place and of the impact which this inevitably has on young people.

The intention of the present government, given powerful effect by a series of Education Acts through the eighties and into the present decade, seems to be fourfold:

1. To revise education standards.
2. To widen parental choice.
3. To extend local responsibility for educational provision

above all by giving enhanced powers to governing bodies of schools.

4. To strengthen central government control over schools by giving the Secretary of State wider power over the National Curriculum and over the purse strings.

The 'standards' issue is complex. Serious discussion is not helped by the tendency in the media to oversimplify in the interests of confrontation and 'news value'. Controversy over the teaching of reading, for example, is not helped by presenting serious educational debate as a dispute between advocates of 'real books' and of 'phonics'; still less by the implication that illiteracy among school leavers is a startling new phenomenon. All teachers of reading want their pupils to graduate as quickly as possible onto 'real' reading material; and the great majority of them use a variety of methods to achieve this end, including phonics where appropriate. And adult illiteracy has always been with us on a large scale. In the days of National Service the army found it a big enough problem to produce its own basic reading scheme[6], and the literacy campaigns of the early seventies spoke of millions of adult illiterates.

This is not to deny that there is a problem and a need. Moreover, unwise education theory and practice can certainly make things worse. But a serious approach to raising standards here will take into account a host of factors which at first glance do not seem to be 'educational'. Thus, in a television and radio culture, the ability to read may not be so important. Fashions in parenting are also influential and we may need to ask questions about whether children are helped to value books and reading by being read to regularly at home. The pressures, too, of the new National Curriculum are seen by some infant and junior teachers as cutting into their already limited time for the essential task of hearing children read.

Christians can become actively involved in this particular area in a number of ways. Church mothers and toddler groups and groups of mothers with infant age children can give support to local schools by themselves reading to children, or reading with them as part of group activities. They can provide schools with additional books – and the schools they should support in this way may not be those nearest home, where their own children attend. There is a powerful Christian case here for targeting needy schools in poor areas where parents do not have financial resources – though help in such situations must always be offered in a servant spirit with no hint of arrogance or condescension. And there are churches which quietly run adult literacy groups.

If in general we are rightly concerned about academic standards, we need to beware of glib, unthinking reactions sparked by media sensationalism. We need to be prepared to dig deeply enough to discover real needs. And we need to be concerned enough to seek ways of helping to meet those needs.

The complexity which I have tried to suggest exists over the issue of teaching reading is present in almost all of the 'standards' controversies. So when we look at debates surrounding GCSE and 'A' levels we need again to probe below the headlines. More course work or less course work at GCSE level? A wider curriculum for the sixteen to eighteen year old's in full time education? As Christians, we *should* be concerned enough about these matters to develop an informed and intelligent opinion. But as individuals we cannot possibly address all areas of national life at the same depth. Perhaps the solution is for many more churches to set up their own 'education groups' to keep abreast of issues and feed their conclusions to the rest of the membership for whatever action may seem appropriate.

As Christians too, we need to be concerned about standards in our schools in the area of spiritual and moral education. This is a concern we share with friends across a wide theological spectrum and also with members of other faith communities. The rising tide of secularism in our society has turned many of our schools into places where it is very difficult for a young person to take religion seriously. Young Christians often find their faith under attack, obliquely or even directly, in an environment where only the affairs of this life are seen as being 'real'.

Traditionally, moral education in our schools has been given in the setting of Christian religious teaching. Not surprisingly, schools which have abandoned any claim to be Christian have not found it easy to find fresh ways of moral education. In many secondary schools, in particular, it would be hard to identify a clear 'line' on morality. The word itself frightens too many people off. In an agnostic society 'tolerance' can become the chief virtue and 'judgemental' attitudes the chief sin. Morals become relative, a matter of personal preference and teaching children the difference between right and wrong becomes a near impossibility. About the time he became Secretary of State for Education, John Patten drew attention to the difficulties for moral education created by the loss of the eternal dimension. 'Dwindling belief in redemption and damnation has led to loss of fear of the eternal consequences of goodness and badness' he wrote among other things[7]. His article attracted some scorn and a good deal of hilarity from educationalists but I have not seen it seriously answered.

Again, it is easy to over-simplify. If young people are not encouraged to consider the possibility that Christianity is true in school, the same is the case in the media and in most homes. It would be unrealistic to suggest that treating Christianity seriously in schools will lead to spiritual revival in the nation. But at the very least we need to challenge the secular trend in schools and seek to keep open a doorway to the dimension of eternity, and an awareness of the Christian view of morality.

For most of us this will be difficult. Our most likely 'way in' will be on a local level, through the schools we are personally involved with as parents or simply as interested members of the community. The spiritual tone and impact of a school will depend very much on the openness of staff to the spiritual dimension. A short discussion on the wonder and mystery of the universe in a science lesson, or the moral dilemmas of the characters in a story in an English lesson, may do more to awaken a child to spiritual realities than a whole year's work in RE. There is no way of accurately predicting outcomes in such matters. Good RE, well taught and given esteem in the life of a school, can be a strong influence.

What is important here, however, is that there is a strong trend towards a schooling which is preoccupied with preparation for this life as seen in terms of career prospects. This can gravely weaken any school's intention to deal properly with its obligation to give a proper weight to spiritual and moral elements.

The government's aim to extend parental choice in the matter of schools is one with which most people will readily sympathise. Real choice is not easy to provide. It implies difference. At a low level this can simply come to mean that locally one school is seen to be 'better' than another. They are both trying to do the same thing, but one is better at producing good examination results, well behaved children, successful sports teams, a high standard of music or drama. These are all achievements which are public and can be measured, and they are all important. But caution is necessary. A school whose pupils come from middle class professional homes starts with an advantage in the examination stakes over a school whose children are from a culturally deprived, poor area. And a school with extensive on-site playing fields is likely to do better in sporting terms than an inner city school which has to take pupils an hour by bus to the nearest shared outdoor sports facilities. Measuring which school is doing a better job is more than a matter of comparing league tables, whether football or GCSE. Choice must involve some kind of assessment and again this must mean getting to know local schools in some depth.

For Christians, the issue of choice is bound up with the question of the spiritual and moral direction of a school's life, which was touched on earlier. For many years while our county schools still tried to be Christian, the importance of this matter was obscured. More recently, as county schools have become more secular, a real choice opens up in many areas between church schools, where the truth of the Christian faith is still taken as the starting point and county schools, both within the national system of maintained schools.

For more and more Christians the question 'What is the faith upon which this school takes its stand?' is becoming important. Again there are many complexities. Not all church schools are clear about their Christian role in the system. And there are differences in how they think of that role. At the same time some county schools continue to have a Christian ethos. But overall a real possibility for choice of a fundamental nature within our schools seems to be opening up.

Church schools do not meet everyone's need for a faith based education. In some areas there are too few of them to provide a genuine choice, especially at secondary level. Over the past fifteen or so years a number of new, usually quite small independent Christian schools have been set up, often based on a particular church, by people who have felt the maintained system is altogether too secular. The numbers involved are small[8], but the movement is significant. This is easier to see when it is related to the growing demand among Muslims and Jews for their own faith based schools[9].

The Education Bill passed at the end of the last Parliament included paragraphs drawing attention to the importance of schools having a clear statement of their basic philosophy. No schools are neutral, and the issue of faith, religious or otherwise, for which a school stands, may be seen in the long run as the most important aspect of the current attempts to widen the scope for choice. Some Christians are alert to this; many more need to be.

In the public discussion of the choice issue so far much more attention has been focused on 'opting out'. This is the process by which schools withdraw from local authority control in every way, and become directly funded from central government. In the wake of the 1992 election many more schools are moving towards this grant maintained status. The intention is that such schools, under powerful governing bodies, will develop as a further strand of schooling, offering another avenue of choice. They will be both more independent and better funded than typical local authority schools, since they will not have to devote a portion of their funds to the upkeep of the local authority's administrative and advisory services. At the same time, they will be more at risk because they will be without a local authority 'safety net' if a governing body makes bad financial or staffing decisions.

The system of 'LMS', local management of schools, by which (since the 1988 Education Reform Act), schools are now taking control of around ninety percent of their finances, while leaving a small proportion to maintain local authority services, may actually offer a better option to most schools.

Questions of choice, however, must be linked with questions of funding. How much money is to be spent on schools, and how is it to be shared out? The greatly increased powers which governors now have over how schools spend their money means that governors, and through them local communities, are in a better informed position to ask whether their schools are actually receiving enough money to do their job properly. This is vital. School buildings need money spent on their upkeep and improvement. Many will claim, with good cause, that too little has been spent on their own local school. Books and equipment cost money and the demands of the National Curriculum now beginning to be felt often mean large scale restocking and re-equipping (eg for science in primary schools). And by far the largest proportion of any school budget goes to pay staff salaries.

Government concern for choice, for a new approach to curriculum, and improved standards may here be in conflict with the long-standing, and perfectly proper government concern to keep education expenditure down. An informed and vocal Christian public opinion must play its part in helping to determine priorities here. And that Christian opinion must itself be shaped by gospel priorities. While we are rightly concerned with the quality of schooling available to our own children, we have a mandate to be more widely concerned for others in the community (Phil 2:4) and especially for those who lack the wealth, the power or the voice to make their own needs effectively known. It is not fanciful, I suggest, to see Jesus' parable of the sheep and the goats (Matt 25:31–46) as having an education dimension 'I needed to learn, and you would not let me be taught'. More directly, the words of Proverbs 31:8–9 summarise much of the teaching of scripture; 'defend the rights of the poor and needy.'

So we may well need to ask whether it is right for the government to spend large sums of public money on a few City Technology Colleges, providing enhanced choice and a better quality of education for a relatively small number of children, while the overall expenditure remains so low that necessary repairs to buildings are put off year after year, or staff cannot be employed for lack of funds to pay them.

What happens in our schools today will have a significant effect on the quality of life in our society in the early decades of the twenty-first century. Above all it will help to shape the attitudes, values and beliefs of the growing generation. In this short essay I have drawn attention to some of the trends in schooling of which we need to be aware if we are to act responsibly as Christian citizens in this area of the national life.

Issues in education are almost always complex. To exercise a proper influence in this field, as in so many others, Christians need to become knowledgeable, prayerful and involved. Recent legislation[10] has made it much easier for ordinary citizens, acting as school governors, to play a valuable part in the work of local schools. Many Christians are active in this way, more could be[11].

Elsewhere I have suggested a range of practical ways in which Christian individuals and churches can co-operate usefully and positively with the good work being done in schools[12]. At the same time it is essential in a society as secular as ours has become, for the Christian minority to be alert to the general direction of education policies, and to be ready, as it becomes necessary, to work to influence those policies. Knowledge, prayer, thought and a willingness to become practically involved are the keys to influence.

For follow up action:

The Association of Christian Teachers (ACT)
2, Romeland Hill, St Albans, Herts, AL3 4ET.
Phone 0727 – 40298
General Secretary: Richard Wilkins
ACT with some 3000 members, is the professional group for evangelical Christian Teachers providing help through its regular publications, and through ACT Now, Spectrum and Digest and through courses run at its centre.

Stapleford House Education Centre
Wesley Place, Stapleford, Nottingham, NG9 8OP.
Phone 0602 – 396270
Director: John Shortt
It encourages Christian thinking and action on all fronts from within the teaching profession.

Christians in Education (CiE) a Department of CARE
53 Romney Street, London, SW1P 3RF
Phone 071 – 233 – 0455
Director: Ann Holt

Speaks more directly to the needs and concerns in education of the ordinary Christian who is not a professional educator. CiE publishes a regular newsletter and operates an education 'helpline'.

Both organisations have a range of useful books and booklets on particular issues.

Notes

1 Section 36 of the 1944 Education Act reads: 'It shall be the duty of the parents of every child of compulsory school age to cause him to receive efficient full time education suitable to his age ability and aptitude, either by regular attendance at school or otherwise.' The last two words established the right of parents to educate their children at home. In the seventies an organisation called 'Education Otherwise' came into being to facilitate home education. More recently numbers of Christian families have been taking up this option and a weekend conference for Christian home educators, the first of its kind in this country, attracted over three hundred people (the figure includes children) in Spring 1992. Numbers involved are still relatively tiny, but this is a growing movement. For more information contact *Christians in Education*.

2 J. C. Pollock *Shaftesbury* Lion.

3 Revd. Spencer Leeson *Christian Education* Longman's Green 1947.

4 In January 1990 some twenty percent of all pupils in the maintained sector, over 1,400,000 young people were being educated in Church based schools, the vast majority of them Anglican or Roman Catholic.

5 The 1944 Education Act established this requirement in all maintained schools. The 1988 Education Act reaffirmed it, with some modification.

6 *Sam is a Soldier*, produced by the Royal Army Education Corps, was an essential tool for many a basic literacy class throughout the fifties.

7 John Patten, 'There is a choice: Good or Evil' *The Spectator*, 18 April 1992.

8 *The Christian Schools Trust*, set up to link such schools, is in touch with some eighty, with a total pupil number of perhaps 5,000. Further information can be obtained from *Christians in Education*.

9 About fifteen Muslim independent schools exist, some of which are seeking voluntary aided status within the maintained system, notably the Islamic Girls' School in Brent. There are already a number of Jewish

voluntary aided schools (twenty-two in January 1990) and others which have sought voluntary aided status so far in vain.

10   The Education (No 2) Act 1986 set out the main changes in the role of the governor under which most schools have operated since September 1988.

11   *Christians in Education* has a mailing list (Summer 1992) of some fifteen hundred known Christian school governors. Undoubtedly there are many more.

12   See the *Christians in Education* pamphlet *Care for your Local School*.

7

The British Afro-Caribbean Community

Joel Edwards

The New Immigrants

On 22nd June 1948, the ocean liner, *Empire Windrush* docked at Tilbury with 492 Jamaicans on board. The date marks a recognisable point at which significant numbers of men and women from the Caribbean and Commonwealth countries arrived to participate in the task of rejuvenating post-war Britain.

Their visibility and the publicity were inescapable and the Black profile in those early years brought a novelty factor to the UK. However, the presence of Black people in Britain predated the *Windrush* by some 400 years. In less noticeable numbers Africans have been a part of the British landscape since the Romans and more significantly during the eighteenth century.

As early as 1601 'blackamoores' were sufficiently evident in Britain to warrant an Elizabethan Proclamation 'that those kind of people' be expelled from the realm. In the eighteenth century, the famous *Somerset Case* in 1772, triggered by the antislavery champion, Granville Sharpe brought the issues of the Black presence to the public attention once more. Even respectable papers estimated as many as 10,000 Blacks living in London forming some 3 per cent of the population. In 1750 Bristol had a total population of 43,275 of which an estimated 5,000 were Africans. Nineteenth century Britain became entirely implicated in the Black cause. The greatest political lobby in Britain's history, led by Evangelicals such as Wilberforce, was the Abolitionist movement which presented Parliament with thousands of petitions and led to the abolition of slavery in 1834. Even the launch of the*Evangelical Alliance* in 1846 was marred by the subject of slavery which polarised the position between the American and British delegates. The movement of Black missionaries from the Caribbean and America through the United Kingdom to Africa was not unusual during this period. Given this background it was not surprising that the first Pan African Congress in 1900 was held in London. During the Great Wars thousands of Commonwealth soldiers gave their lives as British citizens.

The arrival of the *Windrush* signalled a new wave of immigrants but not the first. In later years between the mid 1950s and 1970s thousands of men and women from the Caribbean arrived in the UK by invitation. A combination of poor economic conditions and the shortage of labour provided an attractive rationale for the recruitment of unskilled labour and Caribbeans and Commonwealth citizens came in significant numbers to assist the 'Mother Country' and to improve their own circumstances at the same time. By 1961 238,000 West Indians were resident in Britain: this was the highest total of any collection of West Indians outside Jamaica which then had a total population of 1,609,814. The 1971 British Census recorded 220,000 West Indians born in the Caribbean and 223,000 born in the UK.

Black people who inadvertently responded to an invitation to urbanisation pervaded certain sections of unskilled labour. In 1970, 78% of National Health Service ancillary workers were black. As early as 1965, London Transport employed 3,000 Barbadians alone.

Welcome home brother

It was against this background that thousands of committed Christians came from the Caribbean. In those early days of the Caribbean Christian Diaspora, myths and aspirations about the 'Mother country' abounded. England was the place of affluence where Caribbeans came in order to apply themselves to the acquisition of wealth obtainable over a five year period and to beat a hasty retreat to a sun-soaked villa! It is hard to imagine the intensity of the patriotism with which they 'came over'. I well recall going to a cinema in Brixton as a small boy to watch *Seven Brides for Seven Brothers* (in itself, a very reckless excursion for a Black Pentecostal in the 1960s!). The sense of pride which rose within us as we stood erect at the sound of the National Anthem was matched only by the sense of confusion as all the white people streamed past us to beat the rush. How times have changed. The experience was totally inconsistent with the Union Jack in my Caribbean classroom and the frequent chanting of 'I vow to thee my country'.

But Caribbeans also came with distinct apprehensions about 'Mother'. England became regarded as the place where Christians came to die. The pre-renewal ecclesiastical landscape of the 1950s and 1960s provided little attraction to the Caribbean Christian. Most of them were in fact members of the historic denominations. From the mid 19th Century 31% of church-goers in the Caribbean were Church of England. 29% were Wesleyan Methodists and 17% were Baptists. Even by the 1960s Pentecostalism, which is popularly associated with Black Christianity, was still a minority group and regarded as a 'sect' by social scientists![1]

In fact the 1989 *Pocketbook of Statistics for Jamaica*, showed that 71% of Jamaicans were regular church goers[2].

The proportion of popular church attendance in 1982 was as follows:

Denomination	Proportion of population
Baptist	10.0%
Church of England	18.4%
Anglican	7.1%
Roman Catholic	5.0%
Seventh Day Adventists	6.9%
Methodist	3.1%
Pentecostals	5.2%
	55.7%

(29% non-church attenders)

Clifford Hill's pioneering study of West Indian churches found that in 1961 69% of the population in the Caribbean attended church whereas only 4% of West Indians in London in 1963 were regular church goers[3]. By comparison, the 1989 Jamaican survey mentioned above estimated that out of the total Jamaican population of 2,190,400 in 1982 41% were active Christians. This pattern was underlined by Calley's study which also showed that a smaller percentage of West Indians in England attended the established churches than in the Caribbean, even in areas where Caribbeans resided in relatively significant numbers[4]. England, Hill concluded, did not turn out to be the 'Mecca of Christianity' and he was convinced that 'this was a major cause of many migrants' lapse of faith . . .'[5].

The newly arrived Caribbean Christian community of the 1950s and 1960s participated in the struggles and traumas associated with any immigrant group in a minority situation. It sought for shelter under the canopy of the existing church structures and found little that resonated with its own expression of Christianity. This was not always the result of hostile rejection or polite indifference – although these reactions contributed to the deterioration of faith amongst Caribbeans – but was also the result of a mismatch of cultural responses and an incongruity between the secularised formalities of many churches and the simple fervency of many Caribbeans.

Calley identified 80 West Indian churches in Britain by 1961[6] and in the main these were Pentecostal churches. It is a misrepresentation of Black Church growth to surmise that the inception and development of these groups were due primarily to rejection by 'white churches'. Many 'white churches' made heroic attempts to accommodate others with whom they were totally unfamiliar and which had an identity entirely distinct from their English pentecostal counterparts. Black Churches were not brought into being solely as a result of racism. This would make them entirely a community by default. Whilst God is able to produce good fruits from our bad seeds this is not the whole story! Black Churches came into being to fulfil spiritual, social and cultural needs which would otherwise have gone unmet – and the Caribbean Church in the UK is an indication of God's ability to meet a people's need through their own ministry to themselves.

The seeds of growth development

Immigration had a direct impact on the development of the Caribbean Church in Britain in its more formative years. Roswith Gerloff's recent study highlights the fact that the major church groups were formulated between 1953 – 1960 and coincided with restrictions imposed by the 1962 Race Relations Act[7] However, the early immigrants were totally committed to an indiscriminate approach to evangelism which swept across all cultural boundaries even though it had more cultural affinity with other Caribbeans.

Many Caribbean Christians saw themselves as missionaries[8]. Undoubtedly, most Caribbeans were driven by patriotic and economic considerations but soon came to identify God's purposes in their arrival. As a small boy, one of the Scriptures which became consciously woven into my recollections of church life in the 1960s was from the book of Esther 4:14 'Who knoweth whether thou art come to the Kingdom for such a time as this' (AV).

As the saying goes, 'Birds of a feather flock together'. That is certainly true of minority groups and was true of Caribbeans in the early years. Non-Christians formed small social networks. The Black Christian community was thrown against itself. The Church became a safe and familiar haven of rest. But this was not a negative existence. It provided affirmation, social and cultural identity and a place where they would be educated. The

Church offered a place for spiritual sustenance and vitality. The Caribbean Church community provided the greatest and most life-supporting context for its existence in a hostile or alien environment, not through a contemplative exegetical framework but through 'vital' theology which gave meaning to lives which were often marginalised. Within the community of the saints, life in the 'world' could be reassessed and people were given the will to survive on Monday morning.

Body ministry was lived out rather than verbalised. The 'priesthood of all believers' was expressed rather than thought through. In this community, the testimony of the illiterate man could be as liberating as the sermon from the preacher. There was little debate on the rightness or wrongness of a woman's freedom to preach or exercise leadership. This is not to say that Black women ministers had an easy passage as Io Smith has shown in her own autobiography.[9] However, the Caribbean Church, as a celebration community rather than sacramental community, has always been less preoccupied with fine-tuning theological nuances and has, consequently, had a far more liberating effect on individuals, bestowing a sense of worth and personal affirmation on those who would otherwise go unnoticed.

This personal enhancement was also buttressed by the 'holiness' theology of incipient Methodism which is the theological bedrock of Caribbean Christianity. It expressed and expresses itself in a demand for personal sanctification and challenged Afro-Caribbeans to a life style of ethical certainty in a secular environment of moral indifference and ethical ambiguities. At the heart of Black preaching was the expectation of the Second Coming. Eschatology was not a part of the liturgical vocabulary but it was inalienable from Church life. Essentially, this was not escapism – even if it did produce social detachment from world realities. As the Black American theologian, James Cone, describes it, 'black eschatology existence bestowing wholeness in the present situation of pain and suffering . . .'[10]. A conviction of hope gave incredible strength to individuals who could otherwise have become overwhelmed by their circumstances. Added to this, the Pentecostal heritage from which the majority of Caribbean Christians drew their strength held within it the potential for its future development.

Before church growth systems were popularised in the UK, Black Pentecostalism had a strong code of expectancy which included statistical growth. Pentecostalism, of course, was committed to the idea of 'signs following believers' and 'spiritual results'. It was, perhaps inadvertently, an alternative, intuitive church growth science which required visible proof of the life of Christ in the worshipping community. Things were *supposed* to happen when people met with a living God and worshipped in Spirit and truth and the claims of the Good News were expected to produce optimism and growth in the most derelict and desperate conditions in post war Britain.

Inner city saints

As the urban theologian Ray Bakke has pointed out, 'we have an urban future whether we like it or not'[11]. Caribbeans in general and Afro-Caribbean Christians in particular have a long urban history in the UK. The post-War Caribbean community by its pervasiveness in urban Britain has found its way to the heart of the society although it does not fully enjoy the privileges commensurate with its contribution. Urban conditions inevitably throw up the issues and tension in society in sharp contrast and the Caribbean community has therefore become identified almost exclusively within this context. In the popular media Blacks and Asians are often synonymous with 'problems', 'riots', or 'unrest'. There is a very powerful association of ideas between 'Caribbeans' and 'cricket'; sadly, it also carries over to Task Force, Urban Priority Areas, bad housing, under achievement and crime.

With over 90% of the UK population living in urban areas Caribbean Christianity has been called to participate as partners in the salting of the cities. MARC Europe's 1989 survey *Christian England* has shown that Afro-Caribbean Christianity thrives in the urban areas where Black churches are almost exclusively located. There is a real sense in which the Caribbean Church is where the people live. Its impact as salt and light has not been politicised. It is true that until recent years its involvement on the social and political front was noticeably absent and this has left it open to allegations of irrelevance and political indifference. As we will see, the Afro-Caribbean Church has inevitably become more involved in its community and its relevance-rating is climbing the scale but the vitality of its non-political, preventative action on behalf of inner city people should never be undervalued.

Today the presence of many Black church groups is making significant contributions to the life of its own community in comparison with the wider church community. Black activists who challenge Caribbean Christians about the absence of a British-grown Martin Luther King or Jessie Jackson have overlooked a vital point: it took the Church in the United States over 200 years to produce Martin Luther King Jnr! But they also overlook the fact that effectiveness is not always measurable by political manoeuvres or radical slogans. Salt and light make little noise. Ordinary men and women – many of whom were unskilled – were ill-equipped to relate and interact effectively with the complexities of British political and socio-economic realities. Their energies were spent in surviving the lethal doses of economic deprivation, marginalisation, institutional and personal racism which was a part of their daily diet in urban Britain.

The Afro-Caribbean community has therefore been an integral part of Britain's changing complexion. The remainder of this chapter will attempt to trace the process of transition in the Afro-Caribbean Church with references to some wider issues which have had an impact upon its own development.

The stages of church growth

In my own view, the Afro-Caribbean Church has experienced four periods of transition since the 1950s. Curiously, Roswith Gerloff's work has identified four periods of development between 1952 to 1990 although she has not given clear chronological stages in each case.[12]

1 The inception of the Afro-Caribbean church

I would identify this stage between 1950 to 1965. This was the early period of the early Church dealt with above. If a caricature is permissible it is what I regard as the 'suitcase church' (the 'grip church' in Caribbean vernacular!) which typified the 'short term immigrant' perception of the church community. Most members of the Afro-Caribbean community saw themselves as visitors. They were indeed 'strangers and pilgrims' and content to be so. The 'early church' certainly had no long-term objectives and at the earliest point in this period evangelism was a reflex response borne out of an intense commitment to Christ.

For many Caribbeans, the sense of gripping greyness which greeted these pioneers was summed up by Ira Brooks in his description of his arrival in England in 1956.

> Only minutes had passed since I stepped out of the taxi, but the weight of my battered suitcase and the cold wind had forced me to release my hold on the luggage. I stuck my burning fingers into the pockets of my overcoat and paced backwards and forwards to ensure that blood was still circulating in my veins.[13]

At least Ira Brooks had an overcoat. Many did not. The traumas of job and room-hunting, the unfamiliar cold, strange surroundings and fish and chips from newspapers was the stuff of which homesickness was made. When the Caribbean Christian sang:

> *'I've got a longing, I'm homesick to go*
> *To a land without heartache*
> *No sorrow, no woe*
> *There's nothing but trouble in this world below*
> *I've got a longing*
> *I'm homesick to go'*

he was doing what is now better known as contextualising his theological framework. This was the survival church.

2 The period of consolidation

Between 1960–1975 the Caribbean community in the UK began to think long term. By 1960 Cyril Osbourne's 'Keep Britain

White' campaign, the Notting Hill disturbances, Enoch Powell's 'rivers of blood' speeches and successive Immigration Acts of 1962, 1965, 1968 and 1971 gradually closed the door of opportunity on Caribbeans coming into the UK.

This was also the period when the Caribbean Church grew. Immigration certainly stimulated its growth but did not account for the whole story. Increasingly men sent for their wives and children and stopped sharing rooms as a means of economic survival. Between 1960–1975 the Afro-Caribbean Church experienced significant growth as Afro-Caribbeans realised that they would be here for more than 5 years. During this period many churches developed their infrastructure and began to think long term. The *New Testament Church of God* opened its first full time Bible school in Birmingham in 1963. Growing congregations bought derelict church properties, upgraded their ministerial status and established national Headquarters and autonomy. This was the stage of the 'letterhead' church. Afro-Caribbean Christians were here to stay.

Towards the latter stages a keen interest in social and political issues began to develop. A second generation of indigenous Blacks emerged to challenge and agitate the founders of Black Christianity in the UK. Fanned by the flames of Black consciousness movements from the United States, Black youngsters were emerging from the classrooms to ask questions of their parents and pastors to which they were receiving no answers. Simultaneously, the relativism of the Afro-British culture rose up to test the dogmatism of their parents' 'Caribbeanisms'. Funk music and jazz, new dress codes, alternative ethical norms and contradicting perceptions about discipline exacerbated the 'generation gap' within Caribbean homes. The breakdown of the tenuous family unit had begun. The Caribbean family – a strong concept in the Caribbean – was constantly under attack in Britain. Many parents were forced to abandon their children to grandparents during the 1950s and 1960s. The reunion of a teenage boy with his estranged parents after five or ten years, was often a recipe for domestic disaster. In many homes, overcrowding and poor housing, parents working long unsociable hours and a great gulf between the child's education and the parents' familiarity with the educational system did little to bridge the gulf and provide a bond between the two. The examples of much Black underachievement which appeared in published statistics during the 1980s were sown during this time.

The clash of cultures began to rage in the Caribbean Church during this time. For all concerned, it was a painful but natural development. The struggle was intensified because there were few people able to identify and articulate the problems and those who may have had the skills to do so often lacked official status. Many young Afro-Caribbeans, sad and disillusioned, left the churches in pursuit of an identity with which they could relate. Rastafarianism claimed some. Others simply fell by the wayside, opting out of the church culture in order to redefine themselves in the light of their political and social context.

3 The period of initiation

Ironically, even during some of the most difficult periods of Caribbean Christianity in Britain the Church was experiencing overall growth. MARC Europe's survey identifies a 20% growth in the Afro-Caribbean Church between 1975–79. This third period of transition then, 1975–1985/8, was a very crucial stage as Afro-Caribbeans began to act indigenously within the UK.

The accumulated impact of racism became all too evident by this stage. Within the wider Caribbean community voices rose in protest at injustice and racism. The Commission for Racial Equality instituted in 1976 to replace the toothless Community Relations Commission provided a flow of information which demonstrated the need for change. Racism was rife in the major institutions and reflected itself in employment, housing, education and the criminal justice system. In 1981 68% of all complaints received by the CRE were related to employment. In 1983 the CRE's report showed that 61% of white men with O level GCEs had professional status as opposed to 42% of Blacks and 29% of Asians. A 1980 report on education in London showed 59% of children deemed to be educationally subnormal were Black. The Swann Report of 1985 was merely an extended exercise in confirming what many Afro-Caribbeans had by that time come to know. Within the prison system, over 20% of young adult prisoners in 1982 were Black. Some 40% of children in care were Black.

This is the context in which the Caribbean Church began a conscious attempt to relate to the social realities during the late 1970s and 1980s. Churches which had devised activities for young people and extended their youth programmes to include the wider community through senior citizens clubs, supplementary schools and the like, soon found that it became necessary to understand the workings of local councils and grant aiding bodies in order to obtain financial assistance. Leading figures within the Afro-Caribbean setting were necessarily becoming politically aware even though they were not politically active.

Organisations from within the Black church began to appear. The *Afro-West Indian United Council of Churchs* (AWUCOC) was launched in 1976. In its 1984 Handbook AWUCOC was confident that, 'the lead taken by the Black Churches is like a light in a very dark tunnel, offering to a downtrodden and depressed people hope in this world, and salvation in the world to come'.[14] Aware of the global issues facing the Black people both within and outside the Church, a number of church-based groups sprang into being with a clear commitment to respond to their social and political realities. Increased community involvement brought a new wave of relevance to many churches. The presence of some civic dignitaries during the most important meetings became the rule rather than the exception. This was the 'business card' church.

4 The period of dynamic transition

Over the last five years, Afro-Caribbeans in Britain have undergone a period of dynamic transition. The search for identity has continued – particularly for young Blacks. It would appear that the romantic appeal of Rastafarianism is losing its grip on the Black youth culture and sometimes being replaced by the African-American Muslim influence. Black people can no longer be automatically associated with working class status. The African and Caribbean community in Britain has dared to believe – against all the odds – that it can dream bigger dreams. David Smith, a senior Fellow of the *Policy Studies Institute* believes that in twenty years Black children will be better educated than white children.[15] Today, it is an archaic attitude which struggles with the concept of an intelligent or articulate black person.

Within the Black Community in Britain the crisis of identification remains. It is the challenge to retain cultural continuity with an 'African-ness' which is neither idealistic nor a blind radicalism which bypasses common sense. So often the Black radical becomes incensed by blatant injustice to the point where blackness is more important than the preservation of our humanity and a God-given dignity. Such an attitude leads to a polemical existence where all one's energy is spent in a struggle to survive. It ceases to be *living* and becomes a constant effort to resist suffocation. Bitterness – even with just cause – is unhealthy. After a while it becomes self-destructive – the self victimisation of a people who for too long have been held captive by others. The prisoner imprisons himself in a righteous cause. As the editor of the Black American magazine, 'Essence' wrote recently, 'We must define ourselves by the best that is in us, not the worst that has been done to us'.[16]

The struggle for identity is too important to be handled from an idealistic point of view for it implicates the personhood of African and Caribbean people. A 'sloganistic' lifestyle may fail to rise above the level of mindless rhetoric. In the interests of self-preservation Black youths must seek to rise above the stereotypes which have allowed Africans in Britain only limited access to positions of influence over the last 250 years. Sports and music may be gifts accumulated by a rich heritage but they should not constitute the horizon of Caribbean attainment in Britain. The development of any people group as it responds to and interacts with other cultures around it, must never be loosed from its spiritual moorings. In the final analysis it is a battle for the human spirit.

The Black Church in Britain is the most coherent expression of the Afro-Caribbean community. It is far more influential than is commonly recognised by our secular society. Its work of preservation, social and economic maintenance often goes unheralded. Its intrinsic strength, moral lead and numerical presence has, I believe, earned the respect of many influential bodies. Whilst Caribbean and African churches experience an element of insulation from non-Christian Blacks, this does not entirely disqualify them from adequately reflecting the needs and progress of many Black people in Britain today. It is my view that the developments in the Afro-Caribbean community are adequately reflected in the future development of the Afro-Caribbean Church in the UK.

The challenge to a proper identification is a matter of some urgency for African and Caribbean churches as we approach the twenty-first century. The Black Church must recognise without reservation that there is a place for a legitimate Black consciousness without a reverence of blackness. In fact, blackness is no more sacred than whiteness. Any attempt to weave an indestructible union of all Black people around 'blackness' is an abstract exercise and is doomed to fail. It is a false expectation which reinforces feelings of inadequacy when it fails to materialise. The togetherness which Black people in Britain must explore goes deeper than a colour scheme. It is a consciousness that people of African and Asian descent are consistently undermined by a system which has a vested interest in doing so. The struggle, which may be given poetic licence and described as a 'Black struggle,' has to do with a united opposition to particular acts of anti-human behaviour aimed at people who are black. To insist on an inherent Black identity as a prerequisite to resisting racism is a very long process indeed! The quest for Black identity may be an illusive and non-productive exercise which gives injustice more breathing space. Black consciousness is an exercise in self-affirmation which opposes injustice from the standpoint of a proper evaluation of oneself as a Black person. This appreciation means that one is able to entertain anyone else who wishes to join in the struggle. Even a former oppressor may become an ally. This was certainly one of the important features of Martin Luther King's approach.

Of course cultures do not stand still and the danger of romanticism is that it tends to freeze the past. Romanticism is a poor tool for the management of social change. 'Culturalism', I suspect, may be as dangerous as 'nationalism'. Culture must be *valued* but also *evaluated* against the natural transitions it requires if it is to keep us relevant. Afro-Caribbeans may, some day, have to face up to a reality which says that there is no such thing as *a* Black Culture, although there are black *cultures*. That just makes us fully fledged humans with God's gift of diversity.

To return to the battle against injustice. Amongst the changing trends in Britain in the 1990s is the rising tide of racism. It is often polite, but it is always powerful. Racism is no respecter of institutions and John Root's article, 'Racism in the Church of England' is a timely reminder of that.[17] His work reflects on the Church of England's 'Seeds of Hope' report, published in October 1991. Basically, the report concluded that in many places 'there is only tolerance where there should be welcome and appreciation'. This means that the struggle which many Afro-Caribbean Churches face in dealing with injustices within the historic churches is no different from the struggle against racism in the courts, the police, or white Pentecostalism which emanates from the United States and relates directly to many Afro-Caribbeans in Britain. The battle is the same, even if the terrain is different. In relation to this the community of faith – black or white – must handle 'sloganistic' language with caution. Slogans like 'anti-racist' and 'anti-sexist' are sociological constructions which need examination. With the passage of time, the language will change. Therefore, Christians should concern themselves much more with matters of Biblical justice which directly relate to race and gender in order that their actions will always be Biblically based rather than sociologically determined.

Within the Afro-Caribbean Church many other challenges confront us. Second and third generations of Black Christians are participating in an upwardly-mobile culture within the Church. A rising professionalism has become very evident within many of our larger church groups. Within another generation it is conceivable that 'Black Church' will no longer be synonymous with 'working class deprivation'. The old idea of 'redemption and lift' appears to have visited Black Britain. Champions of the Black Church poverty cause may have to seek an alternative vocation.

Increasingly there is a demand for a more cerebral celebration and the contemplative mode. In the Afro-Caribbean Church Graham Kendrick is becoming vogue. Perhaps this is necessary for survival. The Afro-Caribbean Church which has so far impacted mainly on Afro-Caribbeans is therefore faced with its own identity crisis. The *African and Caribbean Evangelical Alliance*'s Theological Study Group has dedicated a number of workshops to examine this issue which faces the Black Church at a critical time in its development. In a multi-cultural society, Caribbean Christians are engaged in a vital debate to identify the implications of being regarded as a 'Black led' church. The label bequeathed to us by white researchers has been wholly adopted by some sections of the Afro-Caribbean Church in Britain and flatly rejected by others. The label is of course meant to be *descriptive* rather than prescriptive.

At a 1991 ministers conference in Birmingham, Trevor Hall, a black senior civil servant with the Home Office declared his anxiety that, given present trends, Afro-Caribbeans were now 'an endangered species'. If this is true it has very serious implications for African and Caribbean churches in terms of their witness, evangelism and worship culture over the next twenty years. The current challenge facing African Caribbeans in Britain is the need to maintain an identity which is true to its African-Caribbean heritage without becoming a cultural irrelevance to other sections of the community. To a degree Black people have achieved this in popular music and in sports. The same challenge faces Black Christians both within the historic churches and those who belong to the Black Church Community.

Getting there together

Afro-Caribbeans in the UK have been forced to deal with the reality of being a minority culture and surviving within it. As we have seen, the survival has not been without consequence. Black people continue to be significantly over-represented in unemployment, the prisons, mental health and social services residential provisions. The rising tide of racial assaults in inner cities silently continues to scar the face of urban life and the potential for urban unrest in areas where Black-police relations remain volatile is never very far away.

But in the face of all these current trends there is still much scope for a positive work of reconciliation in the UK.

Reconciliation in this respect should never be seen as a one-sided event. It is not the sole responsibility of the host community alone to initiate acts of reconciliation although undoubtedly the major contribution must inevitably come from the host community. It is right that political and academic institutions should set about the task of revamping – by legislation if necessary – the structure which may make others feel that they are legitimately 'at home'. In the same way, Christian institutions have an equally important task. Recent developments to arrest the under-representations of Blacks in leadership roles within the historic churches have been very welcome although there is still a long way to go. In the first place, very deeply ingrained traces of superiority have still to be dislodged in order to make room for further progress. There is a genuine need for establishment Christianity to really come to terms with the fact that 'white is not always right'. There may actually be room to examine the theology of race by which certain historic attitudes inform our theological thinking and therefore shape our church structures and attitudes. Theological xenophobia is a dangerous thing because it sanctifies racial bigotry by appealing to transcendence. It is necessary therefore for British Christianity to continue examining its own attitudes to other cultural nuances in order that it may avoid marginalising those within its borders who are from minority cultures – either by direct or indirect behaviour. Indeed many urban churches have large sections of black people in the pews. As this is not proportionally represented on the platform, the potential for culturally disjointed leadership and marginalisation is greatly enhanced.

I believe that many historic churches must therefore begin with a 'sanctification' of the idea of race. If the 'world' has a warped view of cultural distinctives, the community of faith must lead the way in bringing a Biblical wholeness to our unity in diversity. Within our churches this will begin to happen as we encourage genuine *encounters* with other cultures rather than seeking merely to *assimilate* or *accommodate* them in the singing and sandwich slot! I have often heard it said that Black people need more positive role models to inspire them. This, I suspect, is only a secondary part of the exercise in building the cross-cultural community of faith within the context of the historic churches. First we must examine and dismantle the old ideas which seep through in attitudes, language and liturgies which alienate and disqualify Afro-Caribbeans from stepping into the torch-light of church leadership.

On the whole, it is easy for Black people to be led by white people. It has happened within the colonies and commonwealth countries for many centuries and is natural to a minority experience. Perhaps white church leadership should not be entirely surprised if most Afro-Caribbeans – particularly first generation – 'assume the position' inside the church as well. A quantum leap is required on both sides to break the psychological pattern of many centuries. But it must be done and both Black and White Christians have a positive role to play. In this respect Afro-Caribbeans must be open to the possibility of leadership and to accept a legitimate place in the leadership in the local church which is consistent with personal gifting.

The Black Church community has demonstrated that Black Christians have the ability to lead. It has not been flawless but it has been valid and viable. In the years to come the Afro-Caribbean Church must maximise this role within the United Kingdom. There will increasingly be challenges to the Afro-Caribbean community to re-assess and redirect its role within Britain. First there is the challenge to avoid a reactionary existence. The time for mere *survival* has passed. In the process of *affirming* itself the Afro-Caribbean community must also *extend* itself to the wider community without necessarily sacrificing itself to any non achievable ideals for an a-cultural existence. Having received so much spiritual and cultural wealth Afro-Caribbeans should not be afraid to develop a missionary mentality within the British setting and beyond. In the changing trends in Britain it is not inconceivable that the Eunuch may be privileged to witness to Philip.

Notes

1   Malcolm J. C. Calley, *'God's People' West Indian Pentecostal Sects in England* (OUP, London, 1965). Also Andrew Walker, *Restoring the Kingdom* (Hodder and Stoughton, 1989) p. 209.
2   Timothy and Doroth Monsma (Cities for Christ), 'Jamaica: Models and Needs' (July 1990).

3   Christopher Hill, *West Indian Migrants and the London Churches*, London Institute of Race Relations (OUP, 1963).

4   Calley, *God's People*, p. 119.

He shows, for example, that whereas in Birmingham in 1958 the total Afro-Caribbean population stood at 20,000 only 10 were members of the Church of England (1961 figure).

Comparable figures:

	Afro-Caribbean pop.	C of E members
	1958	1961
Birmingham	20,000	10
Huddersfield	2,000	5
Leeds	2,000	0
London	40,000	69
Manchester	4,500	20

A much higher proportion were Seventh Day Adventists.

5   Hill, *West Indian Migrants*, p. 6.

6   Calley, *God's People*.

7   Roswith Gerloff, *A Plea for British Black Theologies: the Black Church Movement in Britain and its transatlantic cultural and theological interactions*, Part 1, (Peter Lang, Frankfurt-am-Main etc. 1992).

8   See Philip Mohabir, *Building Bridges* (Hodder & Stoughton, 1989).

9   Io Smith, *An Ebony Cross*.

10   James Cone, *God of the Oppressed* (SPCK), p. 159.

11   Ray Bakke, *The Urban Christian* (MARC Europe, 1987), p. 97.

12   Roswith Gerloff, *A Plea for British Black Theologies*, pp. 55–60.

13   Ira Brooks, *Another Gentleman to the Ministry*, p. 9.

14   *A Handbook of the Afro-West Indian Council of Churches*, (Centre for Caribbean Studies), p. 9.

15   Melanie Phillips, 'Surely you can't be the barrister?' *The Guardian*, 1 July 1992.

16   *Essence*, Vol. 23, No. 2, June 1992, p. 5.

17   John Root, 'Racism in the C of E'. *Anvil*, Vol. 9, No. 1, 1992.

8

The British Asian Community

Pradip Sudra

Background

In 'The Economist' in an article entitled, 'Britain's Browns' the author stated that, 'White Britain finds its one and a half million brown Asians confusing. Who are they?'[1] This and many other similar questions have been posed to me from time to time. I believe the reasons for the question are two fold. Firstly, it is an attempt to understand the latest newcomer to this land and secondly, generalisations, helpful as they might be, have become contradictions. This is confusing and therefore any kind of understanding is very difficult. With the above in mind, I will narrate my understanding of the pilgrimage of British Asians. Following this I will present the reason why I believe the Gospel of Jesus Christ is relevant for them today.

Who are they?

The majority of Britain's Asians are from the subcontinent of

India. Whilst it is true to say that, geographically speaking, Asia is much greater than the subcontinent, the sense in which the term 'Asian' is used in the UK denotes those whose roots lay in the subcontinent of India. It is this group of people that the following essay describes.

According to the Indian census of 1971 there are 1,658 distinct languages spoken in India![2] The main languages spoken by 'Asians in Britain', tend to be Punjabi, Urdu, Gujarati, Hindi and Bengali. Other Asian languages are spoken but these five dominate the scene, the obvious reason being that the earlier immigrants were from the Northern Belt of the subcontinent. The statistics regarding the size of each of these communities are educated estimates at best and highly inflated estimates at worst; suffice it to say that the total figure is approximately one and a half million.

Where did they come from

Britain has seen two distinct phases of large scale immigration of the Asian people. The first phase was from the subcontinent between the mid-fifties and mid-sixties. This was encouraged by the news of labour shortages in Britain and pushed by poverty back home. Many were peasants who had never seen a city in their own country, let alone Britain; many were illiterate even in their own language. From Pakistan came Kashmiris, Punjabis and Gujaratis. After the independence of Bangladesh in 1971, small numbers have also arrived from this country.

The second phase of immigration was largely from East Africa and spanned the decade between the mid-sixties and the mid-seventies. This was provoked by the uncertainty of the newly independent states of East Africa and their consequent policy of Africanisation. Unlike the first phase of immigrants, most of whom were poor, the second phase of immigrants were very different. They were well-off refugees from Black-African rule and not fugitives from poverty. In 1969, 65% of Kenya's Asian workforce was white collar and more than a third of these were professionals or managers. Much the same was also true in Uganda.

What religion do they follow?

There are so many varying statistics available as to the size of the different 'faith communities' that it would be futile to speculate further on them, except to say that generalisations in this area are possible when a comparison is made between a linguistic group and a faith. It would be fairly accurate to say that most:

  (i) Gujarati speaking people are Hindus
 (ii) Pakistani Punjabi/Urdu speaking people are Muslims
(iii) Indian Punjabi speaking people are Sikhs
(iv) Hindi speaking people are Hindus
 (v) Bengali speaking people are Muslims

The only place where this generalisation breaks down is when it is applied to Christianity. The Asian Christian population in the UK is estimated at approximately 35,000. Over half this number come from Punjabi/Urdu backgrounds and the rest is made up of every conceivable linguistic grouping.

Conversions to Islam, Hinduism or Sikhism from among the Asian people is negligible although small numbers of the indigenous Anglo-Saxon people have turned to these faiths.

A factor in this mix is that a number of second generation Asians are either nominal in their faith or they have no adherence to any faith community. Having said this, it has to be stated that as the dividing line between culture and faith is very narrow, it is difficult for the second generation Asian to totally avoid religion.

By the rivers of Babylon

As a young child, moving to the UK from the sunny climes of Western Kenya was very adventurous but I realised that it did not take long for the conversations to constantly drift back to thoughts of the good old days. I recalled the excitement of meeting extended family at community gatherings and how everyone would talk of going back to the country of their origin, that is once they had made their fortunes, their children had completed their education or vocational training had been completed.

In this period when we were settling into our new homes, a new environment and a new country, there was a great sense of solidarity. Interests of the wider community came before personal interests; we were all learning to adjust and make adjustments in order to make life as comfortable as possible for us all. This meant the houses built to accommodate one family often saw a second or third family sharing the meagre resources that they had accumulated. Times were certainly hard but as everyone pulled together, it made life bearable. Those who were used to owning their own businesses or working in professional capacities felt humiliated as they worked on factory floors, doing jobs that insulted their intelligence and robbed them of their dignity. Added to this indignity came the abuses inflicted by the right-wing political parties and the unhelpful stereotypes of Asian people as presented by the media. This has culminated in various inner city conflicts with the police over confrontational police methods and also in the execution of Racist Laws. The Immigration Laws of the 1980s bear witness to this.

However, it is precisely this earlier experience which has made the British Asians good fighters (and survivors). In 1972, Idi Amin of Uganda expelled all Asians from that country – penniless, and yet within one decade well over 50% had purchased their own homes and had started to contribute to the commercial life of this country. It is estimated that the penniless Asian community of twenty years ago has a spending power of over £5 billion today!

A community which saw itself as being 'in transit' twenty years ago, no longer mourns or dreams of its homeland as the children of Israel did in Babylon (Psalm 137). They have made their homes here, their families have been raised here, their material possessions are tied up in this land, in fact, there is no other place that they can call home. It is this new setting that we must turn to in order to understand their cultural and religious worldview. Their parents' worldview seems like worlds away for them!

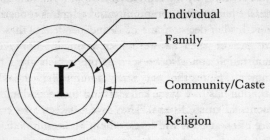

The above diagram of concentric circles best describes the Asian culture. If we start in the centre of our diagram with our focus on the individual, for every decision he/she makes his family would have to be the strongest influence on it. No decision can be made which will adversely affect the family, both immediate and extended. The second level of influence would be the community or the caste. Once personal and family circumstances have been attended to, one's loyalty to community becomes an important consideration. In this respect, it is true to say that only the Hindu has the religious sanction of a social structure for a caste system. Both Sikhs and Muslims would deny that such segregation exists in their communities but in reality it is no different from the Hindu caste system. Finally, it is religion that binds the fabric of society together and becomes the boundary within which one is free to operate.

Generally speaking, this structure is extremely resilient but cracks are beginning to appear. If it cracks it will be a very sad day. The biggest challenge to the above described social structure is the social structure of the host Anglo-Saxon culture which looks something like this:

```
                                           .F

                        .I

   .R                              .C
```

In the host community the individual is an independent unit and whilst he/she has family, community and religious concerns and affiliations, his/her decisions are made independent of these. This structure can be seen as one which gives autonomy to the individual but it can also be seen as one which gives rise to fragmentation, hence the sorry state of our society today! This fragmentation has had a marked effect on the second and third generation of British Asians. They live between two cultures which are often at odds with each other. The result is that they constantly live in a culture clash and for many, their parents' cultural values become submerged. They become people who are neither comfortable in the British culture nor in the Asian culture. The best place is 'in transit'.

The first time that I ever set foot on Indian soil, I was excited at finding my roots but at the same time I lost all sense of belonging. I did not fit into the Indian scene as they treated me as a foreigner and at home in the UK I was being treated as if I did not belong here either. This acute sense of 'non-belonging' is adversely affecting most second and third generation Asians.

Rich man/poor man (divided minority)

On the television programme 'East', screened on 11th September 1992, there was a report on the result of their research on the educational achievements of the Asian community. Their survey revealed trends which we have already alluded to: that whilst in the Asian community at large there has been great upward mobility in the last two decades, this mobility has bypassed those in the inner-city. Gujaratis and Punjabis from East Africa had middle-class backgrounds and were doing far better than Urdu and Bengali speaking people from the Indian subcontinent who came from rural agrarian backgrounds. Again, the Hindus and Sikhs were achieving greater commercial and business enterprises than their Muslim counterparts. A question raised is: 'Is this because Muslims (especially from Bangladesh) were the later arrivals, or is it that they did not have middle-class values to pass on to their children?'

However these statistics are viewed, what is so striking is the great gulf between the various communities. The council estates of Tower Hamlets or any such place where parents are either working in low paid jobs or are on the dole queue, and where the children are trying to study at underfunded schools, is worlds away from the affluence of suburbia where the parents own their own businesses or are professionals and the children are in public schools and are aspiring to study at Oxford and Cambridge.

I have mentioned earlier the division that exists along caste lines. This is a socio-religious system that states that not all men are equal and can be likened to the grand-apartheid of Hinduism. People at the bottom of this scale are often referred to as the 'untouchables'. M K Gandhi, the great Hindu freedom fighter and the father of the Indian nation has said of this system, 'untouchability' is a sin against God and man'.[3] I believe that the essence of this outrage is that we (mere mortals) have placed unequal values on creation, one which God had pronounced to be equal and made in His own image. Sadly, this system is fairly intact and I predict that it will remain so in some form or another for many generations to come.

The indigenous (Anglo-Saxon) culture has influenced the second and third generations in some ways. A specific example is the divorce rate. It is generally accepted that just under 40% of all marriages end in divorce in this country, whereas in the subcontinent the figure is just over 5%. This figure could be inflated if 'living divorces' were taken into account. This is where families stay together for the sake of the children or grandparents. It is also the case when the divorced woman is totally unsupported. Obviously, the woman's position is vastly different in this country in that many women are in good employment and therefore self-sufficient financially. Although a sense of shame is attached to 'being divorced', this is often preferred to a marriage in which partners live separate lives.

Sociologically, the British Asian culture has adopted and adapted itself in order to survive. There is a great resurgence in people wanting to learn more about their roots, their history and their pilgrimage. With this resurgence also come the re-emergence of traditional religions and it is this that we must next turn to.

Religion

As I evaluate the trends over the last twenty years, a pattern that I see taking shape is that in the early years the priority was on settling into a new land, purchasing homes and making one's self comfortable. The next phase saw integration and assimilation in the business sector. The sector to which little time had been given, in the earlier phase, was religion, *but* today it is at the top of the agenda. It seems that the cycle is being completed. By this I mean that attention has been given to 'this world' affairs but whether it is because enough has been accumulated or what has been achieved does not satisfy, the attention has now shifted to 'other world' affairs.

The first area of concern with regard to religion is the size of each of the 'faith communities'. The statistics on these can be very misleading. One way in which this is calculated is, to count the number of Pakistanis or Bengalis in a borough and then project them as the Muslim population in the area. No room is given for classification of other categories such as practising, nominal, lapsed, non-believers, etc. This method of categorisation means that Islam is potentially the largest 'faith community' in the borough and interpreting statistics in this way can give rise to much confusion. Similar pictures can be given of other communities in their own settings.

Leaving aside the issue of the size of the community, let us turn our attention to the state of these faiths (Islam, Hinduism, Sikhism) in the UK. Let me sound a word of warning here. We are not dealing with cults or hybrid derivations or any of these faiths. They are generally not recognised as being within the folds of each of the traditional faiths and are therefore beyond the scope of our present concerns.

It is widely recognised that the 'fall-out' rate from each of these faiths is very high. The main reason offered for this is that it is not another religious philosophy that has won the second and third generation Asians but rather the prevailing philosophy of Materialism. Materialism may not be able to answer all the questions but neither has traditional faith. This has concerned the community leaders greatly and they have responded by calling for cultural/religious gatherings. There is hardly a week when 'pirs' (Muslim holy men), Gurus or Charismatic preachers have not flown into the country for these gatherings. These gatherings are not so much for the purpose of evangelism but a call to the lapsed believers. Where evangelism and conversion occur, it is a by-product rather than through overt efforts at evangelism.

An example of the above was an invitation in the summer of 1992 by the Hindu community in Crawley (mostly Gujeratis) to Moraribapu, a charismatic preacher, for a nine day gathering. He served the community by reading from the Hindu scriptures and then offering a contextualised understanding. Estimates available show that on weekdays approximately ten thousand people went to hear him and this number doubled for weekends. This was a great achievement as the meetings lasted all day and the only seating was on the floor! The lapsed second and third generations formed a sizeable minority of the participants.

Is this a 'flash in the pan' or can we offer answers to questions that many are asking? Is life just health, wealth and prosperity or can we expect to find the answers, not in the material realm but the spiritual? There is a great hunger for spiritual answers, but can this be found elsewhere?

The Gospel as the answer

In this chapter we have been considering the British Asian scene in which I have recounted my pilgrimage and the ways in which my people (ethnically speaking) have been influenced. In this last section I want to offer some answers which I have found, answers which have universal relevance and can certainly answer the questions that my people are asking.

The church

If Britain is confused by her 'Brown citizens' so is the the Church. This issue has created problems of equal magnitude for her leadership in that mission at home and mission overseas were neatly divided into relevant departments. The work of evangelising 'other peoples' belonged to the specialist missionary but as these 'other peoples' are now neighbours to the church members, it is the church members' task to evangelise. Many prejudices come to the surface but a relevant response has not been formulated. In fact, I would suggest that the Church and her training institutions struggle to find effective answers as to how to cope with a society that is now religiously pluralistic. There is no recognisable strategy nor a consensus on the priority of mission!

Looking at the past has not been very encouraging because one is confronted at best by paternalism and at its worst by down right racism. It could be stated that the strongest form of apartheid is not one that is enshrined in the framework of law but one that is etched on the depths of the human heart. What is needed is a new attitude – a new heart. Redemption becomes possible when the words and works of Jesus Christ are followed closely. Ralph Winter has summarised this hope in the following words, 'Christianity is the one religion that has no nationalism at its roots. It is not a folk religion of any one tribe'.

Starting point

It is my firm belief that in spite of material prosperity, Asians are demoralised as there is no hope of a saviour from within their own community. They are turning to the supernatural for answers. In the present climate they are more receptive to the Gospel of Jesus Christ irrespective of their previous allegiances.

The focus has become the person of Jesus Christ, His words and His works. The fundamental nature of the Gospel is such that it has relevance in both developed and underdeveloped nations of the earth. The seed of the Gospel can be planted in Britain where the form is British and likewise the one that is planted in the Asian context will have an Asian form, but fundamentally they are the same.

This adoption and adaptation makes the core of Christian beliefs relevant to all people everywhere. In this respect the Asian believers are coming of age. To date they have been part of what is commonly known as the 'Three Self Movement' (self-governing, self-propagating, self-supporting) but today they are starting to handle the fourth 'self' which makes them truly independent. This is 'self-theologising', where they are not carrying unnecessary baggage, but looking at Scripture afresh and are surprised to find that Jesus is not an alien figure but one who fits into their own setting. He was an Asian immigrant who was a refugee in Africa.

Over the centuries the Western Church has grappled with different aspects of theology and when she has understood it, this theology has been taught through her hymnody. This was only one way in which the people of God (during Bible times) had understood theology, the other way was by telling stories. Jesus himself did this all the time. Story-telling is so central to the Asian culture, and in this context as we start to theologise by communicating the Gospel in a story-telling mode, Jesus begins to make a lot of sense.

In search of that inner peace many of us are like the pilgrims with their saffron robes. In our quest for peace, questions of the way, truth and life have come to the fore. Over twenty years ago I was one such pilgrim who found that I was not pointed to any particular direction to lead me to eternal life but that I was pointed to the person of Jesus Christ. His claims to being the Way, the Truth and the Life are so consistent with everything that He has ever said that today, on my spiritual pilgrimage I no longer wear a saffron robe but I wear a white robe because I am no longer searching: I have found the one in whom I have invested my entire life.

Conclusion

Just under thirty years ago Martin Luther King gave his most famous speech, 'I have a dream . . .'.[4] In this speech he outlined the kind of society that he wanted to live in, one in which his children were not oppressed but treated as equals. A society in which justice undergirded the very foundations of democracy, where people of all races could join hands together and sing in the words of the old negro spiritual, 'Free at last! Free at last!

Thank God Almighty, we are free at last!' I too have a dream. In my dream I see people of all races and colours thronging to meet Jesus. Instead of Justice they have got 'Just-Ice' and instead of righteousness, religion has been poured down their throats. In their oppression and their heavily laden states, Jesus gives them dignity by treating them as His brothers and sisters. He gives them the robe that He is wearing and takes their burdens from them. It is not a pilgrimage to Mecca or Varanassi that lightens their load but rather the tears they see on His face. In my dream I see the Asian people 'Rising above Religion' and worshipping the one who raised them to this new height. There is new found unity and their song is, 'that the lamb might have the reward of His suffering'. My dream is not only for the town in which I live but for every place where my people are enslaved and need to be freed, be that in Tower Hamlets or Birmingham or Glasgow. 'Free at last!' Free at last! Thank God Almighty we are free at last!'

Notes

1   Leading article, 'Britain's Browns', *The Economist*, 29th October 1989.

2   Patrick Johnstone, *Operation World*, (STL/WEC, London, 1987), p. 215.

3   E. Stanley Jones, *Gandhi – the Portrayal of a Friend*.

4   Coretta Scott King, *The Words of Martin Luther King*, (Fount, London, 1987).

9

Popular Alternatives to the Gospel

Ernest Lucas

'Geoff', I said, 'You've been to several Christian meetings with me over the last year. I've explained the Christian gospel to you as clearly as I can. What's stopping you from becoming a Christian?' I was prompted to challenge Geoff like this because I was about to leave the university where we were both undergraduates and I did not know when, or whether, I would see him again. His reply was straightforward and honest. He said, 'I can see that if you accept that the Gospels give an honest account of the life of Jesus then Christianity makes sense. It hangs together. However, if I were to become a Christian now I would have to change my way of life, and I am not prepared to do that'. At least he had done what Jesus said all those thinking of following him should do. He had counted the cost of discipleship and, at least at that point in his life, found it too great.

Eat drink and be merry!

His response is an example of one of the popular alternatives to the gospel – the desire for a comfortable life. Geoff was enjoying the quite legitimate pleasures of student life in Oxford in the 1960s. He was also enjoying the freedom of running his own life the way he wanted to. The idea of anyone, especially God, interfering and, in his view, spoiling his fun was most unwelcome. Putting the pleasures of life, meaning primarily those pleasures which involve our physical senses, before all else – making an idol of them – is called *hedonism*. From time to time there have been teachers who have made this into a philosophy of life or religion. However, for many people, like Geoff, it is no more than a not very well thought out desire to enjoy a comfortable life, without it involving an extravagant life-style. As long as things go along fairly smoothly it is difficult to get such people to take the Gospel seriously. Their only concern is this life and getting the most they can out of it. Talk of accountability to God for how we use this life, heaven and hell and an eternity to come means little to them – until something happens to shake them out of their complacent short-sightedness and makes them think seriously about such issues. A comfortable life like this is something that can be enjoyed only by people who have reached a reasonable level of material prosperity. When the Israelites were about to enter the Promised Land, God, through Moses, warned them of this danger which accompanies increasing material prosperity – see Deut. 8:11–20.

As a result of this link with prosperity, hedonism is closely related to the wider alternative to the gospel provided by *materialism*. This is a concentration on the materialistic aspects of life in this world while denying or ignoring the spiritual dimension. Jesus warned us of the dangers of this when he said:

> Do not lay up for yourselves treasures on earth, where
> moth and rust consume and where thieves break in and
> steal, but lay up for yourselves treasures in heaven,
> where neither moth nor rust consume and where thieves
> do not break in and steal. For where your treasure is,
> there will your heart be also. (Matt. 6:19–21)

It is not only aspiring millionaires who are in danger here. We are all prone to the temptation to set our heart on a better standard of living than we now have. When people make this their idol they then offer their time, energy and talents to achieving it by whatever means seem most likely to succeed. They have little or no time for God because they are too busy 'getting on' in their job by working hard at it, or else they sense that he might demand of them standards of moral behaviour and ways of treating other people that would make it harder for them to succeed in the non-Christian work-place or society. When people like this do succeed and Christians do not, perhaps because of their higher moral standards, godly people are sometimes bewildered. This is nothing new. It is the theme of some of the Psalms, e.g Pss. 10 & 73. In Ps. 73 the psalmist reaches a point of peace when he realises that a relationship with God, which even death cannot take away, is worth far more than material success and plenty which can be swept away at any moment, and will be by death. Ps. 49 expands on this theme with its almost satirical exposition of the fact that the most riches can do for you *in the end* is give you a lavish funeral. Sadly it sometimes takes the death of someone close to them, or the prospect of their own death, to shake people out of a purely materialistic attitude to life.

Does science debunk Christianity?

As well as this popular, practical materialism there is a consciously thought out view of life which is materialistic, based on the belief that matter and energy is all that exists. Those who believe this deny that there is a spiritual dimension to reality. As a result they refuse to believe in God or to accept that Jesus performed miracles and rose from the dead. They appeal to science to support their position. It deals only with matter and energy and over the last 400 years has succeeded in unblocking the secrets of the universe in an amazing way. In the process it seems to have done away with any need for God. This position has been expressed very clearly and cogently by the biologist Richard Dawkins in his best-selling book *The Blind Watchmaker* and his 1991 Royal Institution Christmas Lectures for children, which were televised by the BBC and caused quite a stir in the letters columns of the newspapers. The Christian can respond to this kind of argument in at least four different ways.

To begin with there is the fact, widely recognised by historians of science, that modern science owes a significant debt to Christianity. The founders of modern science, people like Kepler, Galileo and Newton, held Christian beliefs which motivated their scientific studies. They believed that the universe is the creation of a rational God and that they had been made in God's image. They therefore expected that their minds, being finite reflections of God's mind, would be able to 'think God's thoughts after him' and so understand what he had made. The very success of science can be seen as a vindication of these Christian beliefs.

Secondly, it was these Christian founders of science who decided to limit their studies to matter and energy, because these were open to being measured, weighed and counted in observations and laboratory experiments. In limiting their studies in this way they were not denying the existence of non-material spiritual reality. They were simply saying that it cannot be studied by the methods of science. Put simply, science is concerned with *how* the universe works, its *mechanism*. It cannot answer questions about the *meaning* of the universe and life, such as 'Why am I here? What is the purpose of my existence?', 'What is the meaning of life?'. To say that there is no answer to such questions because science cannot answer them is to make a statement of faith about the all-embracing nature of science, which science itself does not support.

Thirdly, Dawkins (like some Christians) makes the mistake of looking for a 'God of the gaps', a God who shows himself in the gaps of knowledge which science cannot fill. As the gaps have disappeared with the advance of science, so has God. This is not the God of the Bible. The Bible speaks of God as not just the *Creator* of the universe. He is also its *Sustainer* (Col. 1:17; Heb. 1:3). What we call 'the laws of nature' are sustained by God. Far from being evidence of nature getting on 'by itself' apart from God, these laws are God's normal activity in nature, an expression of his faithfulness, his reliability. He is free to act from time to time in special ways, miracles, but it is a mistake to expect to find on-going 'gaps' in the laws of nature which are evidence that God exists. The on-going existence of a law-abiding nature is itself testimony to God's existence.

Finally, we have to point people to the historical Jesus as witnessed to in the Gospels. Ultimately our belief in God as Creator, Sustainer, Saviour and Lord rests on Jesus' life, teaching, death and resurrection. The Gospel accounts of this are open to a measure of historical scrutiny by those willing to study them with an open mind.

Humans rule O.K.!

This materialistic outlook is a major part of what is called *secular humanism*, which has been the 'world-view' competing with the gospel in western culture for about the last century. It is called 'secular' because it has no place for God, religion and things spiritual in general. This follows naturally from its materialism. It is called 'humanism' because it is based on the belief that, in the absence of any God, we humans are in charge of our own destiny. As well as being materialistic, secular humanism draws on *rationalism*. This is the belief that the unaided human reason is capable of discovering and deciding what is, and what is not, true. Now Christians should not denigrate the use of our minds. The early modern scientists were right to stress that the human mind is a finite reflection of the mind of God and to have the confidence that the right use of it would lead to an understanding of God's creation. However, there are two factors which limit what can be achieved by unaided human reason.

God is infinite in wisdom and understanding. We are not. We are finite creatures. This limits our capacity to know and understand what God has made. It also limits, to an even greater extent, what we can know and understand of God himself. Some of the pagan Greek philosophers recognised this when they taught that we cannot say definitely what God *is*, only what he is *not*. We know that he cannot be limited as we are, and so we can say what is not true of him, but he is so much greater than we are able to conceive that we cannot say anything positive about him with certainty. There is an even bigger problem. The Bible teaches that we are not only finite, we are also fallen. We are sinners in rebellion against God and that distorts our reasoning (Rom. 1:18) and sometimes blinds us to the truth, especially spiritual truth (2 Cor. 4:4).

All this means that if we are to have any reliable knowledge of God we need God to speak to us himself, to reveal himself to us, and to remove our spiritual blindness. This, of course, is just what the Bible claims God has done. He has revealed himself and the truth about his purposes for us through his dealings with Israel, interpreted by the prophets, and by speaking through inspired Hebrew psalmists and sages. Above all, he has been revealed in the person and teachings of Jesus – the one who was the Word of God made flesh, the Truth displayed in a human being. God has also given us the Holy Spirit, the Spirit of Truth (Jn. 16:13) to renew our minds and enable us to understand the truth (Rom. 12:2, 1 Cor. 3:12 & 13). The fact that through the Bible and the work of the Holy Spirit God reveals to us truth that we could not have discovered using our finite, fallen minds alone does not mean that what he reveals to us is irrational or unreasonable. God is not irrational or unreasonable. His truth often surprises us, frequently stretches our minds and sometimes leaves us groping for understanding. But this is different from saying that it is irrational. When we do grasp and understand it we can see that it all fits together and makes sense.

Much, though not all, secular humanism is optimistic in outlook. It believes that we humans are capable of ruling the world and doing it in a sensible and just way. From where does this confidence come? It can hardly be based on the evidence of human history! It is based in part on the great success of science and technology over the past 300 years. More importantly it is based on an application of Darwin's theory of evolution which goes well beyond anything that can be called scientific. As a strictly scientific theory, evolution seeks to explain how plants and animals can develop and change so that they are well-adapted to their physical environment. Humanists have taken the theory out of its scientific context and used it as a basis for talking optimistically about the probability of human moral, social and political progress. This amounts to turning a scientific theory into a philosophical, even religious, belief. The fact that the scientific theory is misused in this way is no reason to reject the theory itself, any more than the misuse of Christianity to support the Crusades or Inquisition is reason to reject Christianity itself.

It's all relative

Materialism inevitably tends towards a *relativism* in moral values. If there is no Creator God to tell me how to live in order to please him and be happy in the world which he has made, who has any right to tell me what to do? What universal basis is there for moral values? In practice humanists and other materialists often end up appealing to 'enlightened self-interest', but this in fact encourages the view that I am my own 'god' and can do what I like, as long as I can get away with it. The resulting relativism and decline in moral standards has been all too clear in Britain over the last 40 years.

This relativism has been encouraged, and extended to religious beliefs in general, by the increasing awareness that we live in a world where there are several religions competing for our allegiance. This has been partly due to improved communications making people more aware that large sections of the world population are Buddhists, Hindus, Muslims etc. Then, of course, adherents of these faiths have come to live among us. We can see their temples and mosques in our major cities. These other faiths are the popular alternatives to the gospel for the immigrant populations themselves. Some decades ago Christians did not need to study and understand these faiths and how to present the gospel meaningfully to their adherents unless they intended going abroad as cross-cultural missionaries. Now, however, anyone who lives in one of our big cities needs to have some knowledge of these faiths and how to explain the gospel to a Buddhist, Hindu or Muslim.

On the whole the other major world religions have not proved very attractive to westerners. The one exception has been various westernized forms of Buddhism or Hinduism, usually taught by Indian gurus and related to meditation techniques. The most visible of these is the Hare Krishna, or Krishna Consciousness, movement, whose saffron-robed followers can be seen walking busy high streets in groups with their drums and bells, giving out literature and soliciting money and new followers. Interest in eastern ideas began to flourish among the young people involved in the counter-culture movements of the 1960s. It was a sign that secular humanism was beginning to lose its attraction and hold on westerners. Growing ecological problems were casting doubt on the optimistic faith in science and technology. Better education did not really seem to have produced better people. The economic depressions of the 1970s added to the disenchantment.

Follow your star

Possibly one of the most popular alternatives to the gospel, judging by its prominence in the media and the number of people who give it some credence, is astrology – at least in the form of following horoscopes. Astrology is one example of a wider belief in hidden, or 'occult', forces which influence our lives. This belief leads to a desire to understand these forces so that we can cooperate with them, or even control them, in order to succeed in life. The Bible forbids getting involved with such things, and materialism pours scorn on such beliefs. However, the combined influence of Christianity and secular humanism has not completely destroyed belief in astrology and other forms of the occult. One reason may be that astrology promises much for very little cost. Christianity demands total personal commitment to God and the struggle of living in obedience to him in a rebellious world. In return we are promised a great deal in terms of present and future blessing. However, astrology seems a much easier option when it promises blessing (a successful business deal) in return for very little cost (reading your horoscope and acting on its prediction).

Looking for a New Age

The interest in eastern religious ideas and in astrology combine in what has come to be called *The New Age Movement*. The importance of the NAM was highlighted at the 2nd Lausanne

Congress on World Evangelism by Dr Os Guiness when he said that the forces of the NAM 'represent the single greatest opportunity and single greatest threat the church of Christ has faced since apostolic times'. So what is the New Age Movement? It is not a unified movement nor an organised conspiracy. It is a melting pot of ideas. It has many forms and faces. The common factor is a reaction against the spiritual aridity of secularism which is at the same time largely a rejection of orthodox Christianity. Douglas Groothuis describes it as:

> A smorgasbord of spiritual substitutes for Christianity, all heralding our unlimited potential to transform ourselves and the planet so that a 'New Age of peace, light and love' will break forth.

Despite the complexity of the NAM there do seem to be some basic ideas that are widely held by those who identify themselves as 'New Agers'. These are largely drawn from eastern religions, but the influence of western secular humanism has left its mark also. They can be summed up in four words.

1. MONISM. This is the belief that ultimately 'all is one'. The tendency is to stress that this oneness is a unified consciousness. Individuals are all part of this consciousness. It follows from this that the differences we think we see between things are really illusory, a result of our 'unenlightened' state.

2. PANTHEISM. This says that ''all is God'. The unified consciousness is held to be divine. Therefore everything is a manifestation of God. Each individual is innately divine.

3. AUTONOMY. This asserts the total freedom of human beings. Since each of us is part of the divine essence, is 'god', we can do whatever we like. This is meant both in the sense that we have the right to choose what we want to do and in the sense that we have the ability to do it – if only we get in touch with the divine power within us.

4. RELATIVISM. If autonomy rules, I have no right to tell you what is right or wrong for you. Therefore all values become purely relative. You do what you want to, and let

me get on with what I want to do. Moreover, if all differences in this life are unreal, as monism claims, there is no place for such distinctions as right/wrong, true/false anyway. The truly enlightened person rises above these distinctions.

These ideas may seem very strange to you, but they are a mixture of eastern religious beliefs (monism, pantheism, relativism) and ideas drawn from secular humanism (autonomy, relativism).

Like Christians, New Agers recognise that the world is in a mess. They speak of the need for *transformation* for both the individual and the planet. However, for them (contrary to the Bible, e.g. Rom. 3:23–26) the problem is essentially *intellectual* not *moral*. Our problems arise from our blindness to the truth that humans are innately divine and all part of the One that is the ultimate reality. We will be transformed when we *actualize* (make real in our experience) our divinity and unity with the One. Actualization can be brought about in many different ways. The one thing they have in common is the alteration of our state of consciousness so that we realize our divinity and oneness with all things. Some of the methods used are:

- Meditation (yoga, Transcendental Meditation).
- Positive thinking (courses like est, Forum or Lifespring).
- Listening to New Age music with its repetitive melodies.
- The occult (channelling – a New Age term for mediumship, magic).
- Mind changing drugs.

Many New Agers accept the Hindu doctrines of reincarnation and karma. Reincarnation is the belief that instead of just one life we have a series of lives. The 'law of karma' says that how we live *this* life determines our experiences in the *next* life. These doctrines expand the time-scale in which actualization can take place. I may not achieve it in this life, but the progress I make can give me a flying start in the next.

Some New Agers seem to be concerned only with their own personal spiritual transformation. Others aim at global transformation. This, they believe, will happen when a sufficiently large 'critical mass' of individuals have experienced transformation.

While many in the NAM are antagonistic to Christianity, or ignore it, some want to claim that Jesus is on their side. They present Him as an outstanding spiritual master and teacher who was illumined by the universal 'Christ spirit', which can illuminate us all. Thus He shows that we can all become 'christs'. Jesus is said to have gained much of His spiritual wisdom from travelling in the east, especially India and Tibet. He supposedly taught the doctrines of reincarnation and karma. The church censored these from the New Testament. Jesus' death was simply a martyrdom, not an atoning sacrifice (contrast this with Matt. 26:26–28 & Heb. 10:12).

These New Age ideas about Jesus are based partly on the teaching of what are called 'gnostic gospels'. These were written about 100 years after the New Testament Gospels and were rejected by the early church as heretical. They also appeal to revelations received by 'channellers' and documents supposedly kept in Tibetan monasteries. Reputable scholars who have looked for them have never found these documents. The claim that the church removed teaching about reincarnation from the New Testament comes from a misunderstanding of what happened at the Council of Constantinople in 553 AD. It rejected the teaching of a theologian called Origen that the human soul exists before birth in a body. This idea is quite different from reincarnation, a teaching which Origen himself rejected as unbiblical.

Facing the Challenge

The fact that people are turned to New Age ideas rather than to Christ does present us with a number of challenges. We need to examine ourselves. Why are they not turning to the church? To many it seems too like the materialistic, fragmented, secular world which they are rejecting. This criticism should make us take a serious look at ourselves and then act to change things so that it is no longer true. The New Age also challenges us to make sure that we know what we believe so that we can discern between truth and error and share the truth clearly and simply.

Finally, the most effective way to attract New Age people to Christ is to live an authentically Christian life which witnesses to Jesus as the one who is the true source of the peace, light and love which the New Agers say they are seeking. We will then be able to grasp the opportunity to meet the great spiritual hunger of our age. If we are to do this we must avoid paranoia. The NAM is no more or less demonic than secular humanism. New Agers are ordinary, sinful, spiritually blind human beings – who have a sense of spiritual need. Instead of holding them at arms-length we should be offering them the answer to their need in Christ.

Action agenda

1. Make a list of your non-Christian friends and relatives. Prayerfully consider what alternatives to the gospel might be keeping each of them from faith in Christ. This will help you be more effective in sharing the gospel with them and in praying for them.
2. You can improve your understanding of the alternatives, and how to respond to them by reading one or more of the following books:

   D. Cook, *Blind Alley Beliefs* (Marshall-Pickering).

   J. Sire, *The Universe Next Door* (Second edition, IVP, 1983).

   P. C. Moore, *Disarming the Secular Gods* (IVP, 1991).
3. Arrange an evangelistic event to which you can invite a small group of friends and relatives who are attracted by the same alternative to the Gospel. This might be a meal, perhaps a garden barbecue, followed by a relevant talk or video, and discussion.
4. We are all affected by the ideas put across in the media and those of the people with whom we live and work. When you watch TV, read a newspaper, etc try to discern the ideas and attitudes being put across which are opposed to the Gospel. In particular, be alert to the increasing influence of New Age ideas.
5. Prayerfully examine your own ideas and attitudes to see how far you have been influenced by any of the alternatives to the Gospel.

10

The Evangelicals

Clive Calver

Modern society has developed a new game for itself. The popular pastime of 'pigeonholing' people has gained momentum across the coffee tables and newspaper columns of Western Europe. This practice consists of casting a cursory glance over a minority group within society. Having gleaned a minimal amount of information then one proceeds to draw immense conclusions as to how this group functions and what it believes. It is then possible to devise a theoretical box into which they neatly fit. The group is now 'pigeonholed' and can be conveniently understood.

The uncomfortable fact remains that the premises on which these conclusions have been constructed may be far from the truth. Generalisations serve a purpose, but only a limited one. They can create a climate in which society believes that it has now classified a group in terms of its ideology and behaviour; it is surprised when the group fails to conform – and breaks out of the box!

Another scenario is equally possible. Some will come to believe in the image that society has designed for them. They will then endeavour to live up to the expectations that have been created. By so doing they sacrifice their true character. They are contained within the box – and society ensures that it is swiftly battened down.

Such is the dilemma which faces the evangelicals in Western Europe during the closing years of the twentieth century. Having often unconsciously provided grounds for the mistaken impressions of society, the next few years will determine whether the image is to be reinforced, or shattered. This, of itself, constitutes the single greatest challenge facing evangelicals today.

The judgement of society has not hitherto been a favourable one! The tendency has been to view evangelical Christians as:

- a modern-day cultic or sectarian movement.
- a right-wing ideology intent on preserving the status quo in politics and society rather than fostering reform.
- a rigidly fundamentalist group incapable of change, or of handling new concepts and ideas.
- an anti-intellectual faction within the Church which denies the fruit of contemporary scholarship in science and theology.
- a movement which has been imported from the United States engaging in extremes of flamboyance and emotionalism.
- a 'moral majority' movement which exhibits little concern for human suffering or social change.
- a group within the Church, but committed to a rigid belief in scripture, the 'born-again' experience and charismatic worship at the expense of dignity, tradition and orderly conduct.

In short, it is not a very 'British' phenomenon. Its strengths lie in highly impressionable young people and easily manipulated sections of the population.

For evangelicals to regain a position of respect within society they would have to recover their own identity. They also need to engage in a radical re-interpretation of their objectives and beliefs and to emerge from the self-imposed ghettos and the subculture they have created for themselves.

While a Sunday Times article might affirm that, so far as evangelicals are concerned, 'the future belongs to them', the fact remains that few within our society are likely to concur with that judgement. In essence two pathways lie ahead: a broad road of cosy compliance with the expectations of society, or a narrow path of commitment to the recovery of true evangelical beliefs and practice. The former requires little delineation, the latter necessitates a revolution within the evangelical movement. Only a seer could determine which way constitutes the ultimate outcome for evangelicals in Britain at the turn of the millenium.

Towards a genuine Evangelicalism

In order to confront this challenge evangelicals must look backwards, as well as forwards. The desire to recover what has been lost represents a singularly significant trend among many evangelicals today. It possesses a variety of important facets which combine in a significant affirmation – evangelicals must recover their commitment to basic Biblical truths and establish their relevance within our contemporary culture.

The only way?

Our spiritual forefathers maintained the simple Biblical perspective that there is no means by which an individual can encounter God as Father, except through Jesus. But they never had to live and work amidst the plethora of ethnic populations possessing their own indigenous religions. Such is the condition which we possess today. Nor did they have to confront the challenge of the multiple cults and fashionable beliefs which we face, at least not in a prevailing climate of occultic interest, 'folksy' religious ideals and general agnosticism. With so much choice available it seems arrogantly simplistic to affirm that one faith is right, and all the others are wrong!

It is not easy to evaluate what the single most significant issue will be for evangelicals in the latter years of the twentieth century.

Some would point to the continuing debate over Sunday trading, or the growing influence of the New Age Movement. Others would look to the impending struggle on euthanasia. However, the prevailing pluralism of our society must make us realise that the debate over the uniqueness of Jesus Christ will be the pivotal issue for evangelical Christians in the coming years.

On this battleground will be fought the basis for our evangelism and the identity which we seek to maintain. If we concede that other faiths are equally valid, that other saviours exist, or that a person's eternal destiny is determined by other than their relationship with Jesus, then Christianity is reduced to less than its founder claimed and than the Church has traditionally proclaimed it to be.

'Jesus is the only way' may run in the face of modern thinking but it remains the core foundation of Christian belief.

Such an affirmation represents a direct contradiction of popular concepts of tolerance and the general distaste which exists towards any notion of religious bigotry. Our British love of 'fair play' and desire to encourage a sense of 'live and let live', has made us deeply reluctant to assent to the idea that any one faith could be more correct than others.

It is therefore no longer sufficient to merely state that such is the claim of Scripture. We have to learn how to relate the facts of belief to the agnosticism and pluralism of our modern western world in a manner which will enable them to be properly understood. To do this will involve an appreciation of the distinctive perspectives of other faiths. It would surprise many people to discover that their claims are very different from one another, and those of Christianity far surpass the others.

The only truth?

Society boldly proclaims the absence of absolutes while attempting to maintain the rule of law! Truth has become relative to the beliefs of the individual. In other words, we each establish what is truth for us on the basis of what works in our own lives. There is nothing new in this concept, Scripture records that three thousand years ago, they did 'that which was right in their own eyes'.

However, the escalation in popularity of this belief during the twentieth century has bequeathed to evangelicals an alarming problem. If society accepts personal preferences like homosexual practice or spiritual beliefs as being equally valid then the absolute standards of Scripture will be regarded as being invalid. For the majority of our population any idea of 'true truth' no longer exists. Yet society contradicts itself in the insistence that laws are maintained which affirm that some absolutes must be upheld.

It then becomes very tempting for us to acquiesce and allow ourselves to be marginalised by our culture. Instead of maintaining that Scripture represents truth for all humankind, we simply allow ourselves to be convinced that our truth applies to us – others must do as they please. Consequently we are content to claim that the Christian truth is better. The Bible insists that this concept is inadequate. Not only is Jesus 'better', He's unique. Not only is Jesus the *only* truth, but God's way is the *only* way to live in His world.

The only life?

Once spiritual practices and values influenced much of British society. Today such views are sidelined, being regarded as unusual and a matter of personal preference. The materialistic and rationalistic attitudes prevalent in our culture leave little room for spiritual influences.

Secularism has therefore become the dominant creed and religious convictions are given little credence or profile. Where they are valid, as in issues of pro-life, they are greeted as obscurantist and out of date.

Media reaction to Christian attitudes relating to the AIDS tragedy is typically disparaging. Evangelicals are frequently dismissed as reducing this simple issue to the 'judgement of God'. Implied in this assessment is a notion of vindictive deity blindly lashing out in retribution on those who disagree with him.

This is far from the true picture. If I, for example, fill my diesel-powered car with petrol it will inevitably break down. For I have chosen to ignore the manufacturer's handbook and to disregard the maker's instructions. Is this God's judgement on me for purchasing a Renault? Or is it the predictable consequence of my self-determined action?

Similarly, the Christian affirms that God has given the gift of human sexuality, along with guidance as to how it should be employed. Human rebelliousness and disobedience produces tragic consequences. In one generation it was syphilis, in another it was gonorrhoea, then it was herpes, and today it is AIDS. It would be wrong to accuse God, for it is human rejection of His guidance that has created the problem. Furthermore, sin does not merely damage the perpetrators, others suffer – for we live in a corporate society and cannot limit the consequences of our actions to ourselves.

True blame lies in two directions. On the one hand human society can never exclude God. If He truly is the Creator and we fail to live in the manner He intended, then tragic problems will accrue to us. But there is also a sense of guilt for the silence of the Church. If God has revealed His will, in Scripture, for all humankind, then we must reject secular demands that we keep from interfering in society. Instead we need to proclaim God's truth in a manner that others can recognise and receive.

We constantly run the risk of asserting that Jesus only died on the cross as a ransom for us. Instead the Christian message affirms that He died for all who would respond to His call and place their lives in His hands.

When Jesus confronted a Jewish Rabbi He insisted on the need for a spiritual rebirth if life was to be lived as God intended. This emphasis on personal conversion lies at the heart of evangelism and each decade needs to be viewed as an appropriate time for sharing the good news with unbelievers. For if life in Jesus is the only true way then evangelism and witness represent the priority task for each and every evangelical Christian.

The only word?

Undergirding these crucial issues is the traditional evangelical commitment to the authority of Scripture. Here we discuss the framework which God has revealed of His will and purpose for the whole of human society in all generations. It is not surprising, therefore, that there is such conflict over the reliability and adequacy of the Biblical records today. For if the Bible is proved to be false then the objective character of our faith is torn to pieces.

It is in this arena that evangelicals have tended to participate with reluctance in recent years. It is not so much that personal convictions have been shaken, rather that the ability to provide solid evidence for them has often been open to question.

The whole tenor of evangelical doctrines, the deity of Christ, the virgin birth, the Creation, the return of Jesus Christ, the resurrection, the indwelling of the Holy Spirit, all are dependent on the reliability of the Bible.

The fact remains that for the last two hundred years the Bible has been subject to the most intense scrutiny ever given to any manuscript. Despite a multitude of criticisms and theories the argument of its opponents remain unproven. Furthermore, the evidence of archaeology, textual critics and theological scholars is now returning to a more constructive viewpoint, a position that once appeared to be completely out of favour.

Instead of the consensus of opinion favouring attempts to disprove Biblical claims in support of alternative theories, the balance has begun to tilt in the opposite direction.

As ever more outlandish theories have been devised, so the burden has fallen upon their advocates to convince others of the accuracy of their ideas. Once it was the supporters of the Bible that had to support their position, now the pendulum has swung back. An Australian scholar claims that Jesus recovered in the tomb from a swoon upon the cross. He escaped to marry Mary Magdalene. Their union produced two children but ended in divorce. Jesus then remarried, His second wife being a lady named Lydia. They had one child. Finally Jesus dies. While this theory can claim consistency with the cultural milieu of the first century AD, there is not one single shred of tangible evidence that it actually happened! The advocate of this notion has to prove her point and she has signally failed to do so.

Modern rational thought cannot accept the concept of the bodily resurrection of Jesus. So what could have happened? The most popular theory is that the disciples removed the body and invented the story.

Yet, if one logically examines this argument, there are fatal flaws in its reasoning. For if the disciples invented the story then why were they prepared to die for what they knew to be a culpable fiction? If their intention was to convince a sceptical Jewish population, then why did they choose women to be the crucial witnesses to the fact of the resurrection? That would be a sensible procedure in twentieth century western society, but it would have been intellectual suicide in the first century Jewish context. For the testimony of women was not permitted in a Jewish court of law. This would have represented a tragic blunder which must invalidate their case from the very beginning. No sensible conspiracy would fail to marshal all the available evidence, yet stories of Jesus' encounters with Peter and James, his brother, are mentioned in the Bible – but the details are totally ignored.

Faced with objective arguments like these and many others, the case for a deception perpetrated by the disciples is doomed to collapse.

Evangelicals have always been a 'people of the book'. In the latter years of the twentieth century a commitment to the truth of Scriptures must be accompanied by an openness to defend its claims. It is not enough to hide behind a simple acceptance of Scripture, if it is true then no degree of examination will disprove it. As evangelicals appreciate the Bible as truth for all (not just for themselves), they become more prepared to engage in Biblical scholarship. The result is that frequently their arguments appear to be more consistent and reliable than those of their liberal opponents.

Perhaps this has been a major contributory factor in the emergence of evangelicals as a leading force in significant Protestant denominations. Evangelicals have been appointed to positions of senior leadership in major denominations. Fifty percent of Anglican ordinands each year are now evangelicals. Forty-three percent of Protestant churchgoers in England are evangelicals. Something new is happening and a fresh confidence in the Bible as the word of God lies at the heart of this evangelical renaissance. The Apostle Peter spoke of the necessity for God's people to, 'Always be prepared to give an answer to everyone who asks you to give the reason for the hope that you have. But do this with gentleness and respect' (1 Pet 3:15).

To this end the recovery of genuine evangelicalism and its furtherance into the twenty-first century will have to include five key factors. These are:

1. The ability to graciously present in dialogue, argument and debate the fact that Jesus is the only way to meet God as Father.
2. The conviction that Christian absolutes are devised by God for the benefit of the whole of his creation.
3. The determination to share the good news of salvation with the whole of humankind.
4. The confidence that the Bible is not one religious book among others. It is nothing less than the infallible, revealed word of God.
5. The knowledge that real life is only lived under the Lordship and direction of Jesus Christ and in the power of His Holy Spirit.

To this extent evangelicals need to become better theologians! With these commitments in mind the future for evangelicals may well be different to that experienced through the major part of this century.

Towards the practice of Evangelical truth

Having identified the key components of evangelical belief, it is important to ask how they will affect the manner in which we live.

In a world of change

It has been wisely observed that 'constant change is here to stay'.

Evangelicals need to become more aware of shifts within society in order to make an appropriate response. Tom Sine, writing in *Christianity Today*, has commented:

> A leading futurist predicts that we will experience as much change in the next ten years as we have in the

past three decades. Such rapid change means that the church can no longer plan as though the future were simply going to be an extension of the present. We will not only need to do a better job of anticipating the future, we must also become more imaginative in responding to tomorrow's challenges.

Traditionally evangelicals have not been good at change. Yet the current situation demands a re-evaluation of all that we do. Such an attitude is theologically consistent. Although Jesus remains the same, 'yesterday, today and forever', this does not also apply to the operation of his Church.

Whilst we must be diffident about accepting gimmicks, or adopting change for the sake of it, it is vital that we examine what God is blessing at the present time. The Old Testament employs the word 'Ichabod', the glory has departed. We need to determine to continue that which God is clearly using and to ask him if we should stop those meetings, practices and traditions which no longer appear to receive his stamp of approval. In the words of a friend of mine, we must avoid 'unordained' work.

Such an approach is inevitably a radical one. It necessitates church leadership returning their work to God and asking what He requires for the future. This will mean adopting fresh approaches and new priorities – it may also involve abandoning old ones!

The same applies to us as individuals. In the words of the mother of Jesus, we need to 'do whatever he tells you' (John 2:5). This may involve anything from creating new friendships, beginning a new career, discovering different interests or moving to a new location. Some things will not change. Our constant factors are marked clearly in Scripture. But flexibility in non-essentials is critical if we are to change to be culturally relevant to the society in which God has placed us.

In a shrinking world

Contemporary sociologists identify three waves of technological change recorded in history. The agricultural revolution of emerging civilisations, the industrial revolution of the nineteenth century and the major technological and social changes which began in the mid 1950s. The latter wave of change, which is still accelerating, goes far beyond anything that humankind has ever experienced.

Advances in telecommunications have provided us with a sense of existing in a global village. We now possess wide-ranging information from a variety of nations other than our own. Political changes have torn down international boundaries. The development of air transport has given us access to travel to any part of the world.

The implications for evangelical churches are quite enormous. Ignorance can no longer provide us with a convenient excuse for our failure to make our contribution to the mega issues which confront society today.

Media warnings of global warming, famine and persecution now invite a positive response. Ninety-nine percent of the Church's income is still spent on itself. The coming years demand a greater involvement in the field of international relief and development, the release of the persecuted and involvement in issues of environmental concern.

At the same time the potential for mission has vastly increased. The sharing of resources, techniques and personnel between indigenous churches offers new dimensions to change. For the United Kingdom the political realities, post 1992, present Europe as a new mission field. 'Two-thirds world' perspectives now infiltrate and disturb our comfortable thinking. The world shrinks, and the church has fresh opportunities for growth.

In a localised world

As the trend towards the decentralisation of power accelerates, fresh opportunities emerge for the local church. Whatever one's political perspective the basic shift from central government to individual involvement is of great significance.

At an international level the Church has the opportunity to be 'an agent for peace and reconciliation in situations of ethnic and political unrest and a relevant participant in bringing hope, justice, freedom and political help to areas of social need'. (*World Trends* – a report to the World Evangelical Fellowship, 1992).

The same possibility exists in the local community: involvement in PTAs at local schools, Boards of Governors, community enterprise projects, unemployment schemes, homeless projects, prison visitation and many, many others. All are available for evangelicals who are prepared to emerge from their self-imposed ghettos and become involved in the real world.

Our local society will offer a microcosm of the national picture. Family breakdown, the loneliness of the elderly, the needs of the youth and children – all offer the Church a vast range of fresh opportunities.

The fact remains that our response to these situations provides a gateway for the gospel.

In a world without Christ

Evangelism can no longer be confined to the province of a limited number of professionals. Each one of us possesses the potential to be a powerful witness to our faith.

Such an opportunity is not limited to our use of words. We must not be guilty of falling into the errors of our forefathers by allowing ourselves to slip into a false dichotomy, dividing social action from evangelism, and vice versa. Social action apart from the proclamation of the gospel is little more than sanctified humanism.

Evangelism without social action is words without the deeds that illustrate its truths.

One friend told me that he wanted to make a prophetic statement about AIDS. My heart sank because we are so much better at words than actions. I was wrong. A few weeks later we met again and he told me that he and his wife visited the local hospice on a weekly basis. Whilst there they washed the sheets of AIDS victims from their human excreta. It is unsurprising to note that some began to enquire why they did this. Their response was to share the love of Jesus – of such is genuine evangelism and prophetic statements!

The task ahead is an enormous one. The needs of urban and rural areas, the potential for God's people to use the opportunity for secular employment as a mission field, the potential for fresh evangelistic initiatives – all provide the ground for new developments.

Meanwhile the contemporary emphasis on church planting provides further cause for hope. The danger does not exist of neglecting pastoral care, especially of the young and the elderly. If this can be avoided then the goal of creating new Christian communities speaks well for the future.

In a fragmented world

Where nations, cultures and generations divide, evangelical churches can provide an example of united action. With divisions created by charismatic emphases, styles of worship and forms of church government, this will not be an easy task.

However, the desire of Jesus that his people should be united together serves as an instruction for the future. This will only be achieved if evangelicals are prepared to sink their differences and learn from one another. The temptation is there to confine unity to those areas where all will compromise to achieve a 'lowest common denominator'. An alternative exists in the possibility of releasing each other to be what they are in God while combining in mutual agreement on the key issues of our faith.

The long-standing aphorism of Witsius is still relevant today:

In matters essential – unity;
In matters non-essential – liberty
In all things – charity

In facing coming decades evangelicals have to learn a set of practices which are concomitant with their convictions. These build on the previous five trends to produce:

6. Adapting to change in a changing world while maintaining commitment to a changeless Word.
7. Accepting the challenge of involvement in a global situation, contributing to and learning from, those of other cultures.
8. Applying the principles of the Kingdom by engaging in attempts to transform our world. Evangelicals have a fine

tradition of community involvement and the opportunity to recover this emphasis.

9. Actively sharing our faith with those of all classes and cultures who are outside of Christ.

10. Achieving a united sharing across evangelicals of all denominational tribes.

Many questions remain unanswered. Will the charismatic movement continue to make such a major impact? Will evangelicals recover their commitment to social action? Will changes in our national situation create a new climate for evangelism? In these areas uncertainty prevails.

We began by observing that evangelicals are unusual. They are, in Peter's words, 'a peculiar people'. They have always regarded themselves as different from the rest of society, a judgement with which society has frequently concurred.

If an impact is to be made then it necessitates evangelicals establishing the coherence and reasonableness of their beliefs. Then they need to live, with God's help, according to those standards.

If that happens – the future may well be theirs!

The Contributors

SIR FRED CATHERWOOD is the M.E.P. for Cambridge and North Beds. First elected to the European Parliament in 1979, he has been its Vice-President (1989–92), Chair of its External Economic Relations Committee (1979–84) and is currently Vice-Chair of the Foreign Affairs and Security Committee. He has held numerous top posts in industry and Government and is currently President of the Evangelical Alliance. He is married to Elizabeth and has three children.

MIKE MORRIS is International Director of the UK Evangelical Alliance and Executive Secretary of the Religious Liberty Commission of the World Evangelical Fellowship. Married to Katey, a primary school teacher, he lives as part of an extended household in Chichester. He is a member and part of the Oversight Team of Revelation Church.

MARTYN EDEN is Director of Home and Public Affairs for the UK Evangelical Alliance. Formerly, he taught politics and was a member of the team which founded the London Institute of Contemporary Christianity and Christian Impact. With Ernest Lucas he wrote *Being Transformed* (Marshall 1988) and was a contributor and editor of *The Gospel in the Modern World* (IVP, 1991). His wife Janet is a teacher and they have two adult daughters.

JOAN KING belongs to a four generation family and faces the challenge of mid-life with the support of both family and friends. Professionally she is Scripture Union's Family Work Co-ordinator. Her work brings her into contact with families of all types as well as with churches which are concerned to develop their family ministry.

ARKLE BELL lives in Bristol with his wife Sheila, who is a teacher, and their two children, Sarah now a teenager and Philip fast approaching that age group. Since 1984 he has worked for

Frontier Youth Trust as a Regional Field Officer in the South and West. Prior to that he was a Youth and Community Worker in West Sussex and London. This experience has been complemented by academic study for a certificate, a post graduate diploma and an M.A. in youth and community work.

GEORGE OLIVER has taught R.E. and English (1957–70), run a Teachers' Centre (1970–78) and been an Inspector for the Inner London Education Authority (1979–86). Since 1986 he has worked with Christians in Education, which he helped to establish, and has been active in the Association of Christian Teachers. He is also the Convenor of the Evangelical Coalition on Educational Issues.

JOEL EDWARDS was born in Jamaica and arrived in the UK in 1960. After studying at the London Bible College, he worked for 10 years as a Probation Officer. Following a period in the pastoral ministry, he became General Secretary of the African Caribbean Evangelical Alliance in 1988. In 1992 he was appointed E.A. Director of UK Development. He is an ordained minister of the New Testament Church of God.

Joel is married to Carol and they have a son and a daughter.

PRADIP SUDRA is married to Amita and they have a daughter, Maya Ruth. He is presently the Executive Secretary for the Alliance of Asian Christians. For the last 10 years he has worked with the British Youth For Christ.

ERNEST LUCAS is Associate Director of Christian Impact. He is trained in both science and theology. During the last few years he has made a special study of the New Age Movement and written and spoken about it and its challenge to the Church. He is married to Hazel and they have two sons.

CLIVE CALVER is the General Director of the UK Evangelical Alliance. After studying at the London Bible College, he worked as an evangelist (1971–76) before becoming National Director of British Youth For Christ. He then spent two years as Programme Director of Mission England before taking up his present post. Under his leadership, the Alliance has grown to a point where it represents more than a million church-goers from over 20 denominations.

Clive lives in South-East London with his wife Ruth and their four children, Vicky, Kristen, Gavin and Suzy.